mountain bike
maintenance

Paul Vincent

hamlyn

mountain bike

maintenance

EXECUTIVE EDITOR: **JULIAN BROWN**

SENIOR EDITOR: **TREVOR DAVIES**

EDITOR: **ADAM WARD**

CREATIVE DIRECTOR: **KEITH MARTIN**

EXECUTIVE ART EDITOR: **MARK WINWOOD**

DESIGN: **DARREN KIRK**

ILLUSTRATION: **LINE AND LINE**

PICTURE RESEARCH: **CHRISTINE JUNNEMAN**

PRODUCTION CONTROLLER: **LUCY WOODHEAD**

First published in Great Britain in 2000 by Hamlyn,
an imprint of Octopus Publishing Group Limited
2–4 Heron Quays, London E14 4JP

Copyright©2000 Octopus Publishing Group Limited

ISBN 0 600 60063 7

A catalogue record for this book is available from the British Library

Produced by Toppan, printed in China

contents

introd

Get your hands dirty with some real mechanics. In less than 25 years, the mountain bike has gone from an obscure oddity to the most popular form of pedal cycle in the world. The scale of the MTB revolution cannot be overemphasized, and today it is rare to find a household without at least one mountain bike. To the uninitiated, mechanical repairs can be an intimidating prospect, particularly if the target for your spanners and oil is an expensive and gleaming new MTB. Without proper guidance, MTB maintenance can become a frustrating and

uction

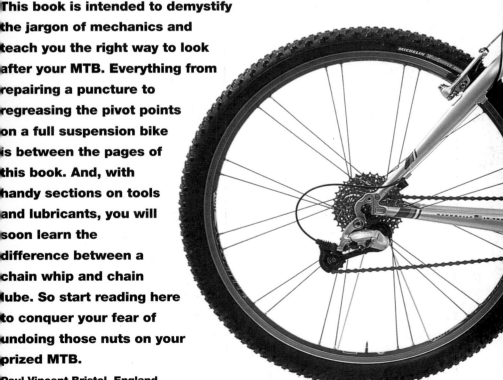

expensive waste of time, however, with the right information, it is a pastime that is not only economical but also rewarding. This book is intended to demystify the jargon of mechanics and teach you the right way to look after your MTB. Everything from repairing a puncture to regreasing the pivot points on a full suspension bike is between the pages of this book. And, with handy sections on tools and lubricants, you will soon learn the difference between a chain whip and chain lube. So start reading here to conquer your fear of undoing those nuts on your prized MTB.

Paul Vincent Bristol, England

anatomy of

Compared to an internal combustion engine, an MTB is a simple machine. The great benefit of this is that it doesn't take much technical knowledge to choose the best bike for you. But you must know your way around the basics.

1. Frame
The double-diamond frame remains largely unaltered since its invention in the 19th century. Even dual suspension frames still use this layout, albeit with a pivoting rear suspension system. Most modern MTB frames are TIG welded.

2. Forks
Nowadays most MTBs come with suspension forks. However, if you have rigid forks on your bike, you can improve comfort by fitting wider tyres.

3. Handlebars
Riser bars were once only fitted to downhill bikes but they are now the most popular handlebars for all MTBs.

4. Derailleurs
The derailleurs are used to shift the chain from one chainring (front) or sprocket (rear) to another. Derailleurs are cable-operated and work by a simple parallelogram principle. The rear derailleur has a tensioning arm to take up the slack in the chain.

5. Headset
The bearings at each end of the head tube that allow the fork to turn in the head tube, and so steer the bike.

6. Seatpost
Seatposts are available in either normal or micro-adjusting types. The size, which is stamped on the side, refers to the diameter.

7. Bottom bracket
The bottom bracket shell houses the axle on which the cranks turn.

8. Chainrings
Most MTBs have threee chainrings, each with specially shaped teeth to help shifting.

an MTB

13. Rims
Rims are usually alloy. Steel rims should be changed for alloy ones as a priority upgrade.

14. Tyres
Tyres are available in many different types to suit a variety of weather conditions. And for those who ride their MTB mainly on the tarmac there are even slick tyres.

15. Brakes
Disc brakes are found on more expensive bikes, but v-brakes have now taken over from cantilever brakes as the MTB standard.

16. Bearings
Bearings prevent friction between moving parts and need regular lubrication.

17. Pedals
Serious MTB riders usually upgrade to clipless pedals that hold the cycling shoe in place like the clip-in bindings of a ski. Traditional clips and straps are also used on MTBs.

9. Cassette
The sprockets are clustered together to form the cassette and can be changed for different ratios. MTBs commonly have between seven and nine sprockets on a cassette.

10. Stem
The stem joins the handlebars to the bike. A high-rise stem is recommended

for those who want a more upright position.

11. Gear cable
Woven steel cable that controls gear and brake operation.

12. Gear lever
Most gear levers are 'indexed', which allows simple click up, click down gear changes.

the roadside

A good cycle tool kit is often the difference between an enjoyable ride and a miserable walk home. In extreme conditions, a few carefully chosen tools can even mean the difference between life and death. Most of all, however, a decent set of tools will save you money and help you learn the art of bicycle maintenance.

Your roadside tool kit should be lightweight and contain all you need to fix common problems and get you home. Check your kit regularly. Tools rust and parts perish if they are not kept dry and well lubricated.

Roadside tool kit

All experienced cyclists carry a few select tools whenever they go out for a ride. A good roadside tool kit should include everything you need to repair a puncture, fix common problems (e.g. broken spokes, broken chain, etc.) and get you home! Multitools are a good way to carry everything you need in one neat package – they usually include the essential chain rivet extractor and selected Allen keys. Whether you choose to carry a Multitool or not, your roadside kit should include the following:

Pump: Don't go for a cheap option here, a decent pump with an aluminium body and chuck will last for years and won't let you down. A mini pump is ideal for bikes where space is taken up with water bottles (the pump is held by clips that attach to the cage bosses). Cartridge inflators are another alternative, and are particularly useful when riding in a group, as they inflate tyres quickly. Remember to take at least one spare cartridge with you on every ride.

tool kit

Spare inner tube: The incidence of 'pinch flat' punctures is high when riding offroad so be sure to carry at least one spare inner tube. If you rely on a puncture repair kit, you should use glueless patches, so that you don't have to wait for glue to dry before applying the patch.

Puncture repair kit: Take a puncture kit, it's good insurance in case you puncture more than once. Avoid using tyre levers unless absolutely necessary as it's easy to nip the tube with them. Make sure your puncture repair kit includes a piece of emery cloth or sandpaper.

Multitool: Multitools, such as the Cool Tool and Park Microtoolbox, take up less space than separate tools and include chain rivet extractors. An absolute must for the MTB racer.

Adjustable spanner: If your budget won't run to a Multitool, the crescent-shaped jaws of the adjustable wrench are more reliable than a cheap metal box spanner. The 6in (152 mm) size will handle all the nuts commonly found on an MTB.

Piece of wire or cable ties: Handy to bind things together in an emergency.

Spoke key: Essential for long offroad tours. If a spoke breaks, the rim will wobble affecting control. A spoke key will allow you to loosen the remaining spokes enough to stabilize the wheel. Some cyclists tape a spare spoke to the chainstay and replace broken spokes on the roadside. Emergency spokes made of Kevlar cord offer an alternative solution.

Oil: On extended rides, you should apply lube to your chain after every four hours of cycling. Small plastic containers of oil take up little space and weigh next to nothing.

A multiple-use tool has all you need in one neat package – carry one wherever you ride.

**The list of tools available for the home workshop is huge...
and growing all the time. However the following tools
should equip you to carry out most everyday repairs.**

the home tool kit

Allen keys: The sizes you'll need most are 5mm, 6mm, 8mm and 10mm. The smaller sizes are available with a 't' bar set-up that enables the user to get a better grip on the tool than is possible with conventional Allen keys. For confined spaces and acute angles, ball-ended Allen keys are best.

Chainring bolt spanner: Used with a 5mm Allen wrench, this little tool enables you to tighten the five nuts that secure the chainrings to the chainset. No other tool can perform this function, so it is essential when the time comes to fit replacement chainrings.

Chain rivet extractor: Essential for changing a worn chain or freeing up a stiff link. Different types of chain require different types of extractor, so make sure you get the right one.

If you want to look after your bike properly, it's worth investing in the right tools. Nowadays there's a growing number of specialist parts with tools to go with them.

Crank extractor: Cranks need to be removed when replacing or servicing the bottom bracket bearings. Some cranks have built-in extractors, but most require the use of a separate extractor tool. Park, Shimano and Cyclo are well-known brands.

Headset spanners: These are only needed if your bike has a threaded headset (usually found on older style or budget MTBs). MTBs with 'oversized' headsets

ABOVE: A workstand is a useful and time saving aid for MTB maintenance.

se the 36mm size. See page
4 for threadless headsets.

in and ring spanners:
Ithough rarely needed, pin and
ng spanners are required if you
eed to make adjustments to the
ottom bracket cups of an older
tyle MTB. The function of the pin
panner is to hold the cup
ecurely while the locking ring is

tightened using a ring spanner.
A ring spanner is used to fix a
threaded ring, such as the
locking ring on an adjustable cup.

Vice: Though not essential, the
bench mounted vice is like an
extra pair of hands. Excellent for
tricky jobs like hub overhauls.

ABOVE: Specialist tools such as these
are required for the removal of worn
bottom brackets and other essential
components.

To a mountain biker there's no more worrying sound than the teeth-jarring whine of metal on metal. Lubrication is what you need to keep the squeaks at bay. A squirt of oil and a dab of grease in the right places will ensure your MTB runs like a... er... well-oiled machine.

lubri

● Apply grease or anti-seize compound to the seatpost to prevent corrosion.

● Suspension frames should be sprayed regularly with mineral oil and should be greased after extended use in wet weather. For full details see page 94.

● Use a lube containing Teflon on the front and rear gear mech pivots and the control cables that serve them.

● Use a 'dry' lube on the chain and ancillary items such as chain tensioning devices and jockey wheels; they're less susceptible to picking up dust than mineral oil.

● Sealed bottom brackets need no maintenance at all, but older units may need greasing once every six months.

● SPD pedals should be sprayed regularly with oil and should be stripped down and greased after extended use in wet weather. Platform and resin pedals should also be greased after a wet ride.

14

cation

Gripshift gear levers require special silicon grease every four months or after every two wet offroad rides. These are the only shifters that require lubrication.

Brake and gear cables require a light mineral oil or a lube containing Teflon oil applied to them after every wet offroad ride.

Most headsets require servicing using a waterproof grease once every six months or after four or five wet offroad rides.

Regularly re-lube the brake bosses using waterproof grease.

All moving parts need lubrication to maintain smooth running, but different parts require different lubes. Many components have seals these days, but they are only partially effective. With extended offroad use, the grease within the parts displaces leaving bearings exposed and susceptible to corrosion if left unchecked.

How often you lube depends on the type of riding you do. Extreme, all-weather, offroad riders should get the oil can out after every ride, whereas pavement poseurs can go six weeks or more without re-lubing.

Suspension forks all require regular lubrication, but the type of lube needed varies according to make and model. See page 86–91 for more information.

Hubs need to be serviced periodically using a waterproof grease. Carefully remove cartridge bearing dust caps and squeeze a little lithium-based grease into the bearings.

pre-ride checks

It's easier to fix your bike at home than on the trail. So follow the nine-point check routine (below and on pages 18 and 19) before setting off.

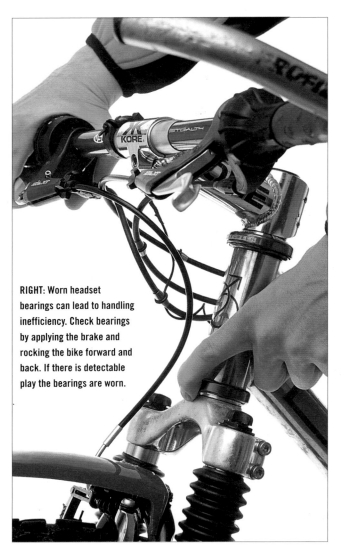

RIGHT: Worn headset bearings can lead to handling inefficiency. Check bearings by applying the brake and rocking the bike forward and back. If there is detectable play the bearings are worn.

1. Brake Blocks

Check brake blocks and disc pads for wear (some brands have wear limit marks). Take into account the rigours of the ride to come and if the pads will be useless at the end of the ride, change them before you set off. The brake blocks on Shimano Deore XT V-brakes can be replaced without disturbing the fitting bolts (see picture top

ABOVE: Turn the pedals backwards and watch for stiff links in the chain. Corroded links should be replaced.

RIGHT: Check brake blocks for wear. The examples shown here are nearly new, but they should still be checked before each ride.

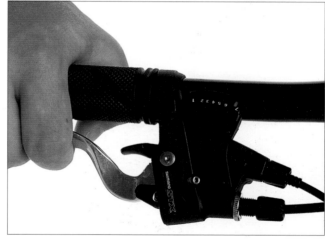

GHT: Test control cables by pulling the levers. If the lever touches the 'ip the cable needs adjusting.

ght), just pull out the pin using iers and slide the old brake lock out of the shoe. Brake ocks come in various grades f rubber; take advice from a eputable cycle shop about 'hich blocks are best for you.

. Brake levers and ontrols

queeze the brake levers hard – they touch the bars/grips, you ill need to improve the cable nsion or inspect hydraulic lines r leaks. If your brakes have arrel adjusters, turn them anti-ockwise. If you don't have arrel adjusters, you must ghten the cables.

3. Tyre tread

Inspect treads for glass or flints that could damage your inner tube. Check tyre sidewalls for abrasions caused by brake blocks. Your safety depends on having good tyres.

4. Chain

See page 46 for chain wear limits, and look for obvious signs of wear such as cracks in those parts of the chain that are in contact with the sprocket teeth and chainrings.

RIGHT: Make sure that wheels are tight. Quick-release skewers turn clockwise.

FAR RIGHT: You should be able to tighten quick-release skewers without the need for any great force.

5. Wheels and spokes

Lift and spin each wheel. If the brakes rub, you will need to check that there are no broken spokes. Spokes usually break at the hub end. Now, true the wheel (see page 34).

Lift and spin the wheels to check that they are running true.

6. Saddle

If your saddle has dropped at the nose, remove the bolt or nut and apply a little grease to the bolt thread. Tighten the bolt or nut using a ring spanner. Check the saddle height and mark the seatpost with a pen – this makes it easy to set the saddle at the same height if you have to remove it.

7. Headset

Apply the front brake and rock the bike forward and back, if there's play go to page 84.

8. Wheels tight

It is essential to be familiar with the correct way to operate a quick release skewer. It is secured by turning in a clockwise direction until it is reasonabl tight, then adjusting the lever position, using the nut on the other side, so that it's in line with the wheel axle. The lever should then be pressed home using the palm of your hand.

Tip

Save time on pre-ride checks with a track pump – they make inflating a tyre easy and most have a built-in pressure gauge. A gauge cuts out uncertainty, so if you don't want to carry a track pump with you a pressure gauge may be a worthwhile investment.

9. Tyres

Don't expect your tyres to be how you left them. Inner tubes lose air gradually and need topping up to between 40 and 50 psi. Follow the maker's recommendations for exact pressures.

Give the tyres a quick squeeze before the ride. If in doubt top them up with air and check the pressure with a gauge.

post-ride checks

ABOVE: Having sprayed the chain with WD40, you must wipe it with a rag and re-lube it.

ABOVE: After you have cleaned the chain, spray it with a water dispersant such as WD40.

A professional chain clean

First you must place your bike on a stand, removing the rear wheel and replacing it with a chain keeper device. Hook the top run of the chain onto the chain keeper, then brush the chain liberally using degreaser. Using a stiff brush, work the degreaser into the space between the sprockets, and leave it to melt the grime for ten minutes. Wash off using copious amounts of detergent and hot water. Finally, use a water dispersant, such as WD40, to displace moisture, then remove any remaining water and dirt using a dry rag. Lube the chain.

After a ride get to grips with cleaning your bike – even if your excursion didn't include a ride through the mud. However, this does not mean stopping at the nearest garage and blasting the bike with a jet wash. These machines operate at such high pressure that water could penetrate the bearing seals. What you should do is...

1. Fill a large bucket with warm water and a little washing-up liquid. Using a washing-up brush, and starting from the underside of the saddle, work down the bike gently running the brush over the whole bike. Flip off the brake straddle wire and run a screwdriver through the gaps in the brake blocks to remove small stones. If mud has dried on the tyres and saddle covering, run the wet brush over them, let it soak in and return to them later. If you're using a high pressure hose (never use a jet wash) avoid the bearings at all costs.

2. Using a separate brush or a chain-cleaning device, apply a solvent cleaner to the chain, sprockets and chainrings. Leave the solvent for about ten minutes to melt the grime. Avoid

splashing solvent on the tyres as this could degrade them. Remove the wheel and hook the chain onto a chain keeper.

3. Return to the tyres and saddle – the water you applied earlier will have softened the mud by now. Rinse off with water and clean the spokes and hubs.

4. Run the washing-up brush along the chain and scrub between the rear wheel sprockets and chainrings using plenty of water. Ensure that there's no mud left on the derailleurs before liberally spraying the moving parts with a water dispersant, such as WD40, to expel moisture, pay particular attention to cables where moisture can lurk. Wipe off any excess dispersant.

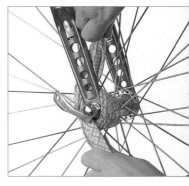

TOP: Worn brake blocks are extremely dangerous. Check them regularly for signs of wear. Badly aligned brake blocks will wear most quickly so keep them well-aligned.

ABOVE: If you must use a powerful hose to clean your bike, you should first protect the bearings with a rag.

Tip

If you haven't got a drain hole in your frame (see Looking after your frame, page 92) lift the seatpost and invert the bike to drain off any water that has accumulated during the ride.

routine wea

Visual checks can help you to assess the wear and tear on your MTB, however, certain components must be checked more closely to determine when they need replacement.

Brake blocks wear very quicky. The examples shown here have hardly been used, but they will need to be checked within four weeks.

Wheel rims

Cyclists are often surprised to learn that wheel rims are gradually eroded by the action of the brake blocks against them. In extreme cases the rim collapses, causing the sidewall to become detached from the rest of the wheel. It is often difficult to determine the precise moment at which the rim should be replaced, so if you are concerned, you should seek advice from your bike shop.

SPD cleats

SPD cleats should be replaced when the click felt as you engage into the pedal becomes indistinct and vague. Cyclists should be particularly vigilant about replacing cleats, as a worn cleat can become unexpectedly detached from its pedal.

Cartridge bearings

During the winter months a close watch should be kept on all components that use cartridge bearings as they are generally more susceptible to

hecks

Chain check

Offroad riding in muddy conditions can quickly take its toll on a bike chain. No part of a bike is subjected to greater strain than the chain, so check it regularly and carefully. See page 46 for more advice on gauging chain wear.

The teeth on this chainring look chipped but are made this way to aid shifting.

the effects of corrosion. Spin the axle of any relevant component and determine whether the bearings feel rough. If the bearings feel rough, you should replace them.

Tyres

Nowadays many tyres have shallow treads, which are designed to shed mud effectively, so detecting tyre wear can often be extremely difficult. As a general guide you should replace your tyres when you notice a distinct change in the way that your bike handles.

money saving tips

Freeing a cleat bolt

When the release and entry of your clipless pedals becomes vague it's time to change the cleats. However, fitting replacement cleats can be hampered if the two fitting screws becoming seized in the base of the shoe. The problem is usually compounded by the Allen key turning in the head of the bolt. To rectify this situation, drill the shank of the screw sufficiently to gain a purchase on the screw.

RIGHT: Using an electric drill and 2mm bit, drill the head down to a depth of about 4mm. Now use a slightly larger drill bit. At this stage the head of the screw will fall off and the remainder of the thread will pass through the base of the shoe.

Stripped mech hanger

In an accident, the rear mech can easily be damaged or even wrenched from the frame, causing damage to the thread that attaches it to the frame. In some circumstances this can be rectified by replacing the hanger retaining screws and fitting a replacement hanger. However, many frames have hangers that are permanently attached to the frame. Fitting a special insert, thus saving the cost of an expensive welded repair and respray, can repair frames with fixed hangers. Ask your local cycle retailer to source the kit parts for you or find a retailer who can do the job using their own kit.

ABOVE: The remainder of the thread is removed using the drill supplied with the kit. The steel insert is fitted to the hanger from the reverse side of the hanger and the mech is attached to it. Use a spanner to retain the nut while you fit the mech to the frame.

tyres

Tyres need to maintain grip, but they must also shed mud from their tread, as this helps to promote a low rolling resistance. Tyres are now available in a wide variety of rubber compounds, so, in theory, there is a tyre to suit every type of terrain and every weather condition.

Pumps

The track pump is easy to use and has a greater capacity than other types. If the pump leaks or becomes difficult to use, take it apart and grease the internal parts.

Inflation cartridges aren't much bigger than a matchbox and inflate a tyre instantly. The body of the cartridge screws into the head of a valve adapter, where a spike simultaneously pierces the seal allowing the gas to escape in a matter of just a few seconds.

The mini pump (See right) is probably the most popular type for general tyre inflation. It conveniently attaches to clips mounted on the bottle cage bosses, though pumping a tyre with one takes longer than other types due to its small capacity for air.

LEFT: MTB tyres come in all manner of shapes and sizes. Soft, coloured, knobbly tyres look great, but are not suited for tarmac riding. Slick and semi-slick tyres are best for road riding. They offer better cornering grip and less rolling resistance.

When riding in wet, muddy conditions, grip is the priority, so tyres with soft compounds and widely spaced 'knobblies' are best. However, on dry, hard surfaces it's important that the bike maintains maximum contact with the terrain. Tyres with shallow 'knobblies', interspersed with a diamond pattern tread, are good on hard slippery surfaces and grass, while a tyre with deeper but closely spaced knobbly tread is best for wet rocks. A harder grade of rubber is preferable for dry, rocky terrain as the riding surfaces are extremely abrasive.

The bead of the tyre is there to hook on to the well of the rim. Kevlar beaded tyres are the best and the most expensive as they are generally lighter.

MTB tyres are available in sizes up to 2.3in (5.84 cm) wide. A fat tyre such as this, offers the shock absorbent aspect needed for the rigours of offroad riding. However, some bikes do not have sufficient frame clearance to allow the use of a 2.3in tyre. It should be noted, that wide tyres are not ideal for long periods in the saddle or when traversing hilly terrain, because of their extra weight.

Get the correct size tyre

The markings on a tyre sidewall are to an internationally recognised standard called ISO – there are two numbers (e.g. 50–559). The first number refers to the section of the tyre, the second is the bead diameter in millimetres.

Get the pressure right

Tyres lose air, so be prepared to re-inflate them if you've left the bike standing for a number of days. Latex inner tubes, which are usually coloured red or orange, are particularly prone to go down between rides as they are porous. Give your tyres a squeeze before you go for a ride and, if in doubt, check their pressure with a gauge.

Straightforward or snakebite?

Puncture repairs that are due to an intrusion (e.g. a thorn) are straightforward. However, those caused by impact (sometimes called a pinch flat or snakebite) are difficult to repair. A pinch flat can be identified by two parallel cuts in the inner tube. Butyl inner tubes are often difficult to repair, particularly if the intrusion has happened adjacent to brand writing that is moulded into the inner tube. In such cases, the patch may detach as a result of being slightly 'proud' of the uneven

BELOW: Puncture repair patches come in a variety of sizes. Measure the puncture (in this case a pinch flat) before selecting the correct size of patch.

puncture repairs

surface. The key is to allow the glue to dry thoroughly before application of the patch.

Repairing a puncture

1. Remove the tyre and tube, then carefully inspect the bed of the rim for sharp objects and any protruding spokes. Replace the rim tape if it's damaged.

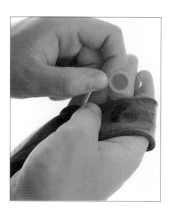

2. Locate the puncture and roughen the surface of the inner tube using sandpaper. Take the time to flatten moulding lines in the inner tube.

3. Apply glue twice to the surface allowing the glue to touch dry between each application. Leave for five minutes then apply the patch firmly to the tube.

4. Fit one side of the tyre over the well of the rim. Inflate the tube so that it's firm, then place the valve through the hole.

5. Working from waist height downwards, work the bead of the tyre over the rim using your thumbs. Check that the tyre bead isn't bulging out anywhere.

6. Finally, inflate the tyre to the recommended pressure.

ABOVE: Fit one side of the tyre over the well of the rim and work the bead of the tyre over the rim using your thumbs.

TOP: If you're using glue, make sure it's touch dry before applying a patch.

LEFT: The markings on your tyre sidewall should tell you all you need to know about your tyre. In most cases recommended pressures and dimensions are clearly displayed.

RIGHT: A freewheel is a user-maintainable item. Worn bearings in the freewheel will accelerate wear and affect the way the gears operate.

servicing a freewheel

Grade of job: Moderate

Tools: centre-punch, hammer.

The threaded hub and associated freewheels are only generally found on cheaper mountain bikes and older bikes. They can be immediately identified by the fact that there is no outer locking ring to retain the smallest sprocket. The advantage with a freewheel type hub is that the components can be taken apart to replace the bearings and, unlike a freehub, it can be oiled easily.

1 Leave the freewheel on the wheel, and with it facing towards you, place the point of a small centre-punch into the right hand of the two holes on the face of the freehub (**See right**). Using a hammer, hit the punch with a short sharp blow. The ring will loosen in a clockwise direction. Always wear eye protection when using a hammer.

2 Place the palm of your hand over the freewheel and turn the wheel to a horizontal position and place on the ground. The bearings and tiny pawls with their springs will fall out. Be careful not to lose the pawls as replacements must be ordered specially by a shop.

3 Using grease to hold the bearings in place, fill up the bearing tracks of each side of the sprocket. Fit the pawls and their springs. Wrap a piece of cotton thread around the pawls to hold them down over the springs.

4 Place the sprocket assembly over the threaded centre section (**See left**), and be careful not to dislodge any ball bearings as you do so. Then place any circular shims over the centre section followed by the locking ring, which tightens in an anti-clockwise direction. Use the centre-punch and hammer to tighten the locking ring.

5 If the freewheel feels rough, you will need to remove the locking ring and lift one of the tiny thin shims from the freewheel body. Screw the block over the wheel in a clockwise direction.

6 Pour a little oil into the freewheel unit, stop pouring when the lubricant issues from the other side.

the shimano

Moisture penetration and subsequent corrosion is the factor that most determines the life span of a freehub. Particular care should be taken when washing the bike; avoid jet washes at all costs. The freehub body (the sealed unit that holds the sprockets) is attached to the main part of the hub. If the freehub feels rough when you turn the sprockets, the bearings have probably rusted and the freehub body will need replacing. In extreme cases of corrosion, the sprockets will turn independently of the wheel.

Cassette hub cutaway

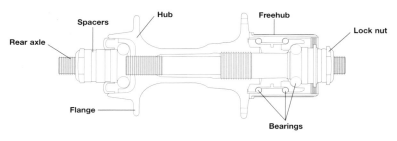

Hub
Spacers
Freehub
Lock nut
Rear axle
Flange
Bearings

Stripping a Shimano hub

Grade of job: Difficult
Tools: two cone spanners, 10mm Allen key, vice, spanner

1 Place the left side of the wheel on the ground then remove the axle. Hold both cone spanners in the palm of one hand. Squeeze them together to loosen the locknut and cone. Remove the bearings. Clean the hub's bearing surfaces and the cones with a rag. If the left-hand bearings' cup surfaces are pitted throw the hub away. If all is well, go straight to point three below.

2 Remove the cassette. Insert a 10mm Allen key into the freehub

end of the hub, and turn it anti-clockwise to remove it – it should be replaced with the same make and model of freehub.

3 Fit the replacement freehub and carefully screw on the hollow fixing-bolt. If it is a tight fit, you have crossed the thread.

4 If the cones show any sign of pitting, renew them. Always use new bearings – the cost is small and

When you remove a freehub, check the plastic spoke protector for damage. If it is coming loose it should be replaced.

freehub

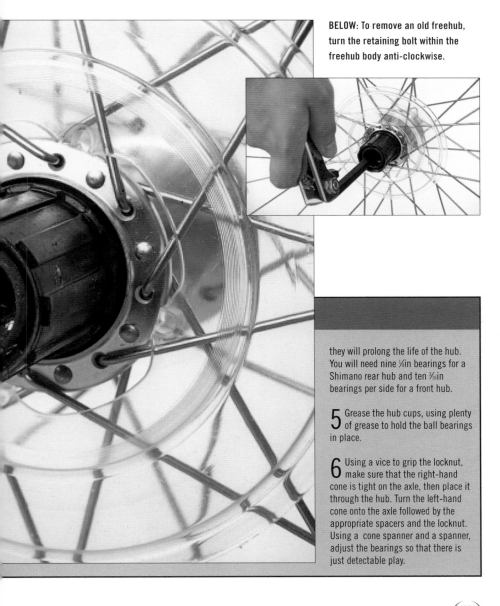

BELOW: To remove an old freehub, turn the retaining bolt within the freehub body anti-clockwise.

they will prolong the life of the hub. You will need nine ¼in bearings for a Shimano rear hub and ten ³⁄₁₆in bearings per side for a front hub.

5 Grease the hub cups, using plenty of grease to hold the ball bearings in place.

6 Using a vice to grip the locknut, make sure that the right-hand cone is tight on the axle, then place it through the hub. Turn the left-hand cone onto the axle followed by the appropriate spacers and the locknut. Using a cone spanner and a spanner, adjust the bearings so that there is just detectable play.

replacing a

Grade of job: Difficult

Tools: lockring tool, chain whip spoke spanner, pen, Blu-Tack, matchsticks.

The first sign of a broken spoke is the rubbing of brake blocks on the wheel rim. Close inspection will usually reveal that the bent part of the spoke, called the elbow, has snapped, leaving the remainder of the spoke to move around while still attached to the nipple. Replacing a spoke on the rear wheel may necessitate the removal of the cassette cogs, as they can often restrict access to the spoke holes (for how to remove a cassette see page 48).

1 Remove the cassette cluster using a lockring tool and a chain whip.

2 Deflate and remove the tyre. Remove the protective rim tape.

3 Take the remains of the spoke to a bike shop and ask for a replacement.

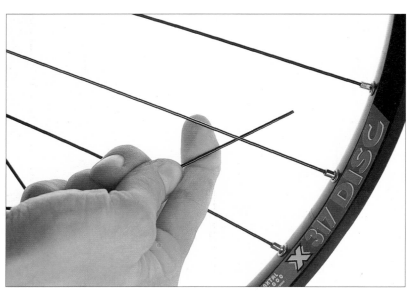

4 Thread the new spoke through the flange hole in the hub, copying the method used on the adjacent spokes. You may need to bend the spoke a little to fit it.

spoke

5 Pass the nipple through the rim and turn it a few threads over the spoke. Now tighten the spoke so that its tension is roughly the same as the adjoining spokes.

6 Far cheaper than using a full wheel jig is to use two matches and a little Blu-Tack to hold them in place. Position the matches so that they are in line with the rim both from the top and the side.

7 If the wheel becomes egg shaped you have tightened a group of spokes too much. Locate the offending spokes and loosen them until the wheel becomes round.

8 Viewed from above, observe the points at which the rim touches the pointers and mark them with a pen. If the rim moved to the left, turn the spoke adjacent to the wobble in an

anti-clockwise direction in order to equalize the tension between left and right hand spokes.

9 Seat the spokes by pressing them firmly with your thumbs. Finally, go back to making minor adjustments to the rim so that it runs true.

lacing a wheel

Grade of job: Difficult
Tools: spoke key, pen, Blu-Tack matchsticks.

Building a wheel may seem a daunting prospect but it is possible. The key is to remember that there are two sets of spokes: the pulling ones, which drag the rim round, and the pushing spokes, which face the opposite way to the direction of rotation. Spoke holes are angled for the left and right hub so you need to establish which spoke to put in first. You must also leave adequate space for a pump hole.

Key steps

1. Place the inboard spokes through alternate spoke holes on the drive side of the hub.

2. Put the first spoke through the hole adjacent to the valve hole, followed by each subsequent fourth spoke hole in the rim.

3. Place the inboard spokes into the other side of the hub – viewed across the hub – place the first of these to the left of the spoke in the opposite flange. Now turn the hub so that the spokes are angled away from the valve hole.

4. Place the outboard spokes into the remaining holes in the drive side of the hub, then place

Put the first spoke in the hole adjacent to the valve opening in the rim.

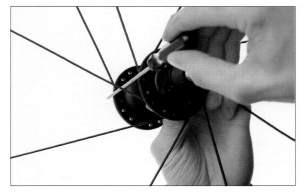

LEFT: The spoke nearest the blade of the screwdriver is slightly behind the one positioned on the opposite side of the hub.

BELOW: Use a nail or a pin held in place with Blu-Tack as a guide.

he first of these under the crossing spoke and place it into the hole two places to the left serving that side of the hub.

5. Do the same for the emainder of the spokes, then urn the nipples until the spokes are held lightly under tension.

Spoking patterns

There are two ways to build a wheel: crossing the spokes, where each spoke is crossed by one, two or three others; and radial spoking, where the spokes radiate from the flange. The former provides an even load on the hub flange and an even pull of torque through the rim. The latter pulls directly on the hub flange, placing greater demands on the hub and rim, so the apparent weight saving of using shorter spokes is often lost by the need for a stronger hub and rim. The three cross pattern is the most reliable.

ABOVE: Short arm mechs (left) provide fast, direct shifting, but they are only suitable for smaller gear ratios. Long arm mechs (right) are commonly found on MTBs.

BELOW: The two screws on the back of the rear mech limit the amount that the mech moves.

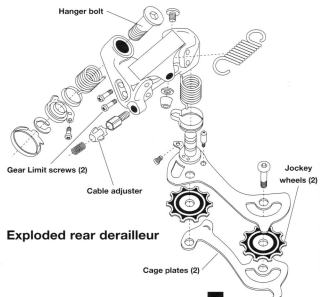

Hanger bolt

Gear Limit screws (2)

Cable adjuster

Jockey wheels (2)

Cage plates (2)

Exploded rear derailleur

rear mech

The rear derailleur (or mech as it is popularly known) draws the chain across the sprockets, shifting from cog to cog courtesy of a cage-and-pulley system. The rear mech is available in many types but those intended for mountain biking are generally longer to account for the wide range of gear ratios on offer.

Anatomy of a rear mech

The top bolt attaches the mech to the frame and contains a spring-loaded arrangement that brings the chain into tension.

The uppermost screw, situated behind the mech, controls the distance between the upper pulley wheel and the first gear cog.

The limit screws control the distance through which the mech travels. Turning the screw anti-clockwise increases the throw in both directions.

The barrel adjuster (shown being turned in the picture,

f the gears become noisy, use the humbwheel adjuster to tension the :able. Turn it anti-clockwise until the 1oise disappears.

With the lower jockey wheel removed the mech is now separated from the chain. Worn jockey wheels can be replaced in this way.

The limit screws on the back of the rear mech should only need adjusting if you change the cogs.

above) determines the indexing performance of the gears. Turning the adjuster anti-clockwise increases the amount of tension exerted on the control cable.

Repairing the rear mech

It is usually possible to repair a rear mech at the side of the trail. A bent derailleur can be temporarily straightened using bare hands. Such a trailside repair, however, will only be good enough to get you home and will need close inspection before your next ride. It is common, in such cases, to

discover that the plates that support the jockey wheels are twisted. The best way to solve this situation, is to remove the plates and straighten them in a vice. Another common rear mech problem is that of the poorly adjusted derailleur. This can usually be resolved by adjusting the limit screws, which control how far the mech travels for the chain to hook onto the first gear sprocket.

Tips

• In the event of a crash, a spoke protector (a round disc that fits behind the cassette), will prevent the mech from being caught and possibly broken by the spokes of your rear wheel.

• If excessive wear is evident in the jockey wheels, replacements can be obtained.

• If you are replacing your mech with one of a different length, you may find that you need to alter the length of your chain. Make sure that the chain works on the largest gear before you hit the trail.

The front derailleur rarely gives problems if adjusted correctly. The most common fault is that the chain unships itself due to incorrect adjustment of the gear limit screws. Problems can also occur when the limit screws seize up due to corrosion.

front mech

BELOW: High and low screw adjuster make it easy to get your front mech working properly. Be subtle with your adjustments though, a half turn can make the difference between a jammed chain and smooth change.

Adjusting the front mech
Grade of job: Easy to moderate
Tools: 5mm or 6mm Allen key, pozidrive screwdriver.

1. Shift the gear control to select the smallest chainring. Turn the cranks and look at the gap between the mech and the largest chainring. It should be between 1–2mm. Loosen the fixing bolt and adjust for height.

2. Viewed from the top, the front mech must be at the correct angle to work properly. The rear part of the parallel plates (sometimes referred to as the cage plates), needs to be 2–3mm further towards your ankle than the front part of the cage. As you tighten the clamp bolt, the mech may twist; compensate by towing the cage plate outwards even more before tightening the bolt again.

3. Inspect the gear outer cable for cracks in the casing, especially at the ends. Replace any metal cable end caps that show signs of splitting. Inspect the gear inner cable for corrosion, especially where the cable is directly exposed.

Tip

Front mechs don't need replacing very often, but if you are unlucky enough that yours breaks, don't be tempted to buy a new one by mail order, as there are many types. Replacements are available in either top-pulling or bottom-pulling types and for several sizes of frame tubing.

4. Turn the barrel adjuster on the gear lever in a clockwise direction when viewed from the front. Clamp the inner cable to the gear mech, but leave some cable slack in the case of Shimano STI, and no slack in the case of gripshift changers.

5. If you haven't got a workstand get someone to hold the rear wheel off the ground. Operate the gear lever; if it's slow to shift the chain onto the middle chainring turn the barrel adjuster at the end of the control cable anti-clockwise until if shifts cleanly. If it's slow to shift back down to the small chainring, adjust the inner gear limit screw by

turning it anti-clockwise. Put the rear gear in the smallest sprocket and shift the chain onto the large chainring. If the chain rubs on the front gear mech turn the screw nearest the crank arm anti-clockwise until the chain is silent.

BELOW RIGHT: Keep the front mech and its moving parts clean and well lubed. The peg on the chainset stops the chain from becoming entangled if it falls off.

BOTTOM RIGHT: If you have to remove a worn or damaged mech, don't split the chain; remove the screw at the back of the mech instead.

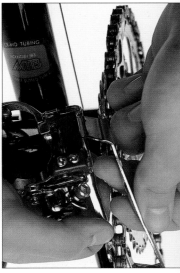

LEFT: Packs of cables that come with all the appropriate fittings and washers are a worthwhile investment.

cables

Gear cables may seem insignificant, but even the best shifters are rendered useless by cheap or ineffective cables.

The standard cables which come ready-fitted to a new bike are adequate for dry conditions but easily corrode when subjected to wet weather. As a result, it is important to lubricate such cables after each wet ride. If, however, lubricating cables does not appeal, you could alternatively invest in one of a growing number of branded maintenance-free cables. These innovative cables work by means of a special seal that effectively cocoons the control wire, protecting it from the elements.

Fitting a replacement brake cable

Grade of job: Moderate

Tools: pliers or cable cutters and Allen keys.

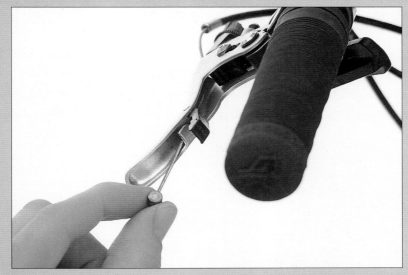

1 Release the clamp bolt using a 5mm Allen key.

2 With Shimano controls, it's easy to access the cables. Lift the black lever towards the grip and withdraw the old cable.

3 Make a note of which slots are occupied by which sections of outer cable. Unhook the old cable to use as a guide to trim the new one. A purpose-made cable cutter is the best device for trimming cables, but pliers can also be used.

4 Fit the outer cables before fitting the red central sleeve between them, then slide the new inner cable through the handlebar control lever.

5 Clamp the inner cable to the V-brake arm using a 5mm Allen key. Cut the cable about 5cm below the clamp bolt.

6 Finish the end of the cable with a cable end-cap and crimp it using a pair of pliers or cable cutters.

gripshift

The gripshift gear-change system is popular with both recreational riders and downhillers. The advantage of this system over rivals (e.g., traditional thumbshifters or Shimano's Rapidfire system), is that the rider maintains a constant grip on the handlebars throughout.

The rider rotates the grip to change gear, moving it towards himself to select a lower gear (i.e. a gear that is easier to pedal) and twisting it in the opposite direction to engage a higher gear. The system is not as robust as Shimano's Rapidfire set-up, but gripshifters are extremely light.

RIGHT: Some gripshifts require the cable to be looped around the barrel of the unit.

Servicing a gripshift
Grade of job: Moderate
Tools: pliers or cable cutters and Allen keys.

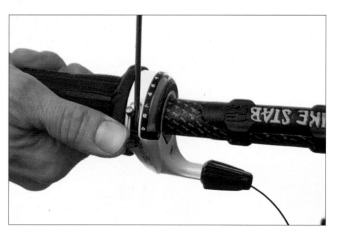

If there's one shifter that needs to be carefully maintained it's the gripshift. Regular greasing is the best way to ensure that a gripshift's index system remains trouble-free.

1 Remove the grips using a long screwdriver and either washing-up liquid or a spray lube. Coat the screwdriver blade with the lubricant and work it round between the grip and handlebar before yanking the grips.

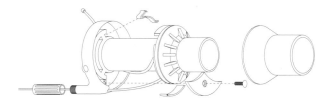

Exploded grip shift

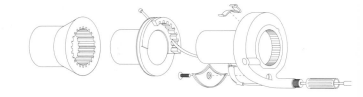

2 Remove the cable retaining plate.

3 Separate the gripshift using a 2.5mm Allen key (older units may require the use of a screwdriver). Clean all parts using diluted washing-up liquid, or gripshift solvent, and a toothbrush. Pay particular attention to the indents around the barrel.

4 Liberally coat all mating surfaces with Vaseline or silicon lube. Offer up the barrel to the housing and replace the retaining screw.

5 Replace the cable. On newer units this involves simply threading the cable through the hole. However, on older units you must loop the cable once round the barrel and through the adjuster, gently pushing the grip shifter barrel into the housing and over the indent spring. You may have to push the cable home with a knife blade before the barrel will press home. Attach the cable retaining plate and tighten the cross-headed screw.

6 Place the separating washer between the gripshift and the handlebar grip. Spray the handlebar and the inside of the grip with airspray or a dry lube.

7 Position the brake levers and tighten the clamp bolts. Set the gripshifters so that there is at least 4mm between the barrel adjuster and the bottom of the brake lever. Tighten the Allen screw just enough to prevent movement.

8 Slide the outer cable section onto the inner cable and re-attach the inner cables to the gear mechs. Check that all the clicks are there. Adjust the gears using the adjuster barrels on the gripshift (**See below**) and the rear mech.

RIGHT: Use the upper part of the chain rivet extractor to free off a stiff link; gently turn the lever until the link is free to move and no more.

chain

The chain has the unenviable task of transmitting your efforts through to the rear wheel. It is also exposed to trail-born muck and grime, so it is vital to keep it both clean and well oiled. Chains are made up of rollers, plates and pins. They are available in different widths to account for the 6, 7, 8 or 9 speed rear cogs that are available. Chains generally need changing every four months. An old chain can accelerate sprocket wear.

Checking your chain

Grade of job: Easy

Tools: rivet extractor, chain cleaner.

1 Using a biodegradable solvent, thoroughly clean the chain, then dry it.

2 Examine the chain for signs of wear. If you notice a definite trough in one of the rollers, you will need to replace the chain. If in doubt, use a Park chain checker (**Above**) to gauge wear. Alternatively, you can measure a section of chain with a ruler to determine wear. Measure from the centre of any pin to the centre of the pin approximately 12 inches (30.48 cm) away. If the pin is at less than 12 1/16in (30.64 cm), the chain is fine, if it's between 12 1/16in and 12 1/8in (30.8 cm) consider replacing the chain, and if it's at 12 1/8in or more you should replace it immediately.

3 If you have to remove a non-Shimano chain, use a chain tool but don't push the pin all the way through. Push it just enough to separate the chain. Don't drive out the black pin that is found on Shimano chains.

4 To rejoin the chain, use a chain tool to press the pin through. In the case of a Shimano chain, fit a special black pin through the ends and press it home using the extractor.

5 On non-Shimano chains the link you have joined will be stiff. To cure this, use the upper part of the chain tool or simply flex the chain until the link is free to move. Check that the pin protrudes equally from either side of the chain.

cassettes

When new, the chain's rollers sit comfortably on the sprocket teeth and spread the load evenly. As the chain wears, the load is concentrated in certain areas, which causes further deterioration. If you let this go on too long the sprockets become hooked, and if you try to put a new chain onto hooked sprockets it will jump. Replacing your chain at regular intervals can slow the wear process down. You may find that your chain has worn too far for a new chain to be compatible with your cassette. The symptom is a skipping chain, and a replacement cassette or freewheel is the only answer.

Changing a cassette

Grade of job: Moderate

Tools: chain whip, lockring tool, spanner, extractor to

1 Clean the chain and the spaces between the sprockets with degreaser. Leave the cleaner for several minutes to melt the grime, then wash it off with a washing-up brush. If you need to use a hose, wrap a rag behind the cassette to prevent any water getting into the cassette body and spray with a moisture dispersant after washing.

2 Check the sprockets **(Left)** for worn teeth. The largest sprocket is usually the first to take on a slightly hooked appearance.

3 To remove the cassette cluster **(Below)**, place a chain whip on the middle sprocket and put the extractor tool into the end of the cassette – use a large spanner for extra leverage. Bear down on the spanner and chain whip to release the lockring.

4 Place the new cassette over the cassette body, screw on the lockring and tighten using the extractor tool.

5 Using the old chain as a guide, split the new chain at the same rivet and thread it through the jockey wheels. Join the chain and free off the stiff link using the chain tool.

6 Check that the gears are working properly before riding the bike.

bottom bracket

The bottom bracket is known as the 'big end of the bicycle' and has the largest bearings on the bike. It is also the mechanism that carries the force of your efforts through the cranks and chain to the rear wheel.

Most bikes now use one-piece bottom brackets, which require no adjustment of the bearings after fitting. One-piece units are very reliable and extremely resistant to corrosion, though the use of a jet wash is to be avoided as any water that gets into the unit is impossible to get out. Some older and budget bikes still come with cup and axle bottom brackets, but it is best to replace these with a one-piece cartridge unit at the first sign of roughness.

Measure the overall distance of the bottom bracket to establish the axle length you require.

Fitting a cartridge unit

Grade of job: Difficult
Tools: 8mm Allen key or 14mm socket wrench, adjustable spanner, crank extractor, bottom bracket removal tool

1 If you're removing a Shimano cartridge unit, undo the shoulderless cup first, turning it in an anti-clockwise direction. Loosen the right hand cup by turning it clockwise. However, if the unit has a grey or black plastic shoulderless left-hand cup it is important to remove the other side first

2 Don't put grease on the axle tapers as it makes it easy to slide the cranks on too far.

3 If the cranks regularly come loose, it's likely that the tapers are damaged. Inspect them; if a taper is swaged at the edges, replace it.

4 The bottom bracket cups on Italian frames loosen in an anti-clockwise direction. Make sure that the bottom bracket fitted to such a frame is fastened firmly.

5 Before you ask your cycle shop for a replacement bottom bracket, measure the overall width of the old unit and the width of the bottom bracket shell on your bike. On MTBs, the shell is usually 68mm, although 72mm is also used.

BELOW: A specialist tool is used to remove the bottom bracket. If one cup is plastic, remove it after first loosening the other side.

the chainset

Chainsets are fitted onto either a taper or a splined axle. Tapered axle cranks should be tightened to a maximum torque setting of 22 ft/lb. A torque wrench that will do this job can be purchased fairly cheaply though you will also need a socket set and an Allen key adaptor for this job.

Tip

When replacing chainrings, you should measure the distance between each of the rings you remove. That way, you can fit spacers to achieve the same set-up as you had before.

LEFT: Use a 5mm Allen key to fit and remove the chainring bolts. The chainrings are retained by the 'Spider', in this case coloured red.

BELOW: The backs of the chainring retaining nuts should be held using a special Shimano tool, as shown here.

ABOVE: The black chainring is an example of extreme tooth wear, while the lower is a new replacement chainring.

Changing the chainrings

Grade of job: Moderate

Tools: 5mm and 8mm Allen keys, crank extractor, 14mm or 15mm socket wrench, torque wrench, Shimano chainring nut tool.

Replacment chainrings are available for chainsets fitted with 5mm Allen bolts. Cheaper MTBs have riveted chainrings that require the whole chainset to be replaced if one ring becomes worn. Shimano and Sugino chainrings have a worn appearance even before they have been used. This irregular design, which incorporates bent and cutaway teeth, is intended to help the chain ramp the gears smoothly.

1 Clean the whole drivetrain using degreaser. Check whether the rings need replacement. A bent tooth is easy to see and can be straightened using an adjustable spanner.

2 Measure the distance across the bolt fixing points.

3 Turn the 5mm Allen-headed fitting bolts anti-clockwise to loosen them, then remove the crank arm using a crank extractor. Remove the worn rings from the chainset spider.

4 Place the new chainrings over the crank spider. If you're changing the middle ring fit it so that the nut is

flush. Holding the back of the nuts, turn the Allen bolts clockwise until finger tight. Now use the special Shimano chain-ring nut tool and a 5mm Allen key to fully tighten the bolts.

5 Fit and tighten the crank onto the axle using a torque wrench.

6 Set the front mech high and low gear limit screws.

7 If the chain hesitates or jams between the chainrings, measure the distance between the chainrings again. Fit spacers behind the middle chainring if the chain drops or slips between the middle and inner chainrings.

cranks

Your cranks require very little maintenance but should still be regularly inspected, with particular attention paid to the area onto which they attach to the bottom bracket axle.

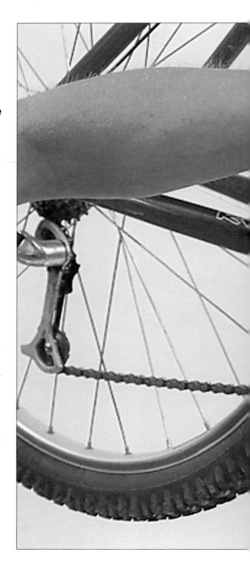

Care should be exercised when removing and refitting cranks during a bottom bracket service. A common error made when removing the cranks is for the extractor tool to twist in the crank end causing damage to the fine threads. A good bike shop will be able to repair this fault, but you should prevent its occurrence by ensuring that the entire thread of the extractor is screwed into the cranks before attempting to remove them.

The practice of using grease on the crank tapers should be avoided as it can cause the crank to go too far onto the axle. In addition, the use of a torque wrench takes the guesswork out of tightening the cranks on to the axle. Most makers recommend 20-23 ft/lb, and it's worthwhile following these guidelines to avoid overtightening and damage to your cranks. Shimano have adopted a splined axle design for their offroad chainsets. Fitting instructions for these chainsets are available from Shimano agents, and should be followed to ensure that the splines are fully engaged with those on the axle.

Some cranks have what is called a 'one key release' and can be removed without the need for special tools. An Allen key is all that's needed to undo a single bolt on the end of the crank arms.

lloy cranks need regular checks to ensure they are tight.

Strong, steel cranks are favoured by specialist dirt riders.

If you use the correct tools, removing the cranks is a simple job. The wrong tools, however, can cause irreperable damage to expensive aluminium bolts.

the V-brake

This is the natural progression from the cantilever. It uses one continuous cable – rather than a cable and straddle wire – to draw the brake arms together, so the compression on the brake arms is more direct than it is with a cantilever.

Fitting a Shimano V-brake

Grade of job: Moderate.
Tools: 5mm and 6mm Allen keys, pozidrive or flat bladed screwdriver, grease.

1 Make sure that the kit is complete and that the package
has not been disturbed. The documentation includes a full
parts list as well as excellent fitting instructions.

2 Fit the special bolt and be sure to locate the washer
properly. Observe the instructions written on the side of
the brake blocks.

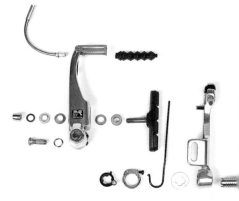

3 Put the concertina seal over the cable that lies between
the V-brake arms and anchor the cable by tightening the
5mm Allen bolt.

4 Change the spacer washers if the concertina seal is
compressed or there's less than 39mm between the arms.

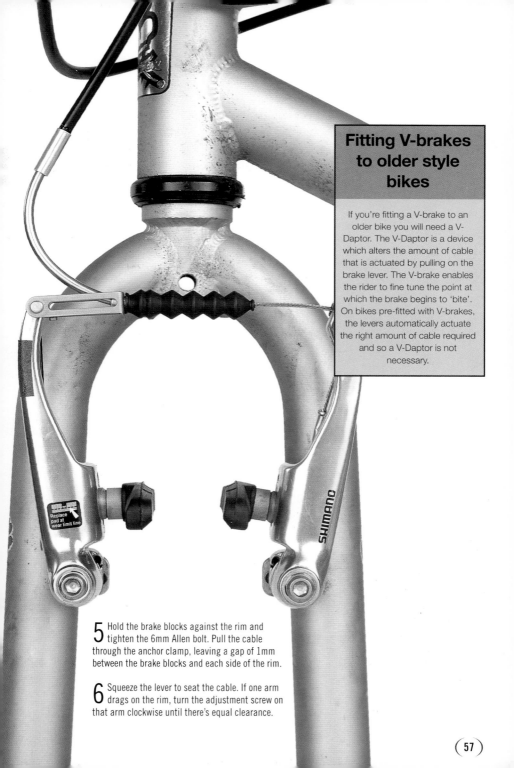

Fitting V-brakes to older style bikes

If you're fitting a V-brake to an older bike you will need a V-Daptor. The V-Daptor is a device which alters the amount of cable that is actuated by pulling on the brake lever. The V-brake enables the rider to fine tune the point at which the brake begins to 'bite'. On bikes pre-fitted with V-brakes, the levers automatically actuate the right amount of cable required and so a V-Daptor is not necessary.

Replace pad at wear limit line

5 Hold the brake blocks against the rim and tighten the 6mm Allen bolt. Pull the cable through the anchor clamp, leaving a gap of 1mm between the brake blocks and each side of the rim.

6 Squeeze the lever to seat the cable. If one arm drags on the rim, turn the adjustment screw on that arm clockwise until there's equal clearance.

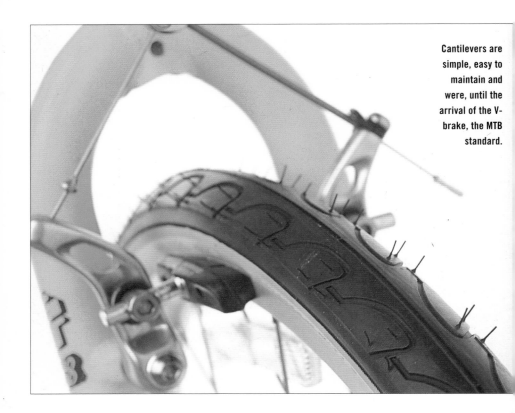

Cantilevers are simple, easy to maintain and were, until the arrival of the V-brake, the MTB standard.

cantilever brakes

The brakes are the most important part of your bike, particularly if you ride offroad on a regular basis. Regular checks and replacement of worn parts should be carried out to ensure that you have safe brakes. The cantilever brake is simple, easy to maintain and has long been favoured by mountain bikers. 'Cantis' also weigh less than other types of braking system. While cantilevers have largely been superseded by more powerful V-brakes on new bikes, the braking systems on older MTBs can work almost as well if properly maintained and adjusted.

Fitting a cantilever

Grade of job: Easy to moderate

Tools: 5mm and 1.5mm (for Shimano) Allen keys, spanners (8mm, 9mm and 10mm), cable cutters, cone spanners (for Dia Compe cantilevers).

1 Remove the cantilevers from their bosses and clean the mating surfaces. Grease the bosses before fitting them back on. If a spring is visible, place it through the middle of the three holes adjacent to the boss. Once tightened the cantilevers should turn freely. Position the brake blocks with the arrows (where present) pointing forwards and square to the rim then hand-tighten the securing nut.

2 Turn the brake lever adjuster fully clockwise then inspect the brake inner cable. If it's damaged, make sure you grease the new inner cable before threading it through the outer section – use the lined variety if you're replacing a damaged outer cable and don't forget to fit metal end caps.

3 Slide the inner cable through the straddle clamp and fit the straddle wire through the anchor bolt on the cantilever. The straddle wire makes up a triangle - the squatter the triangle the stronger the braking power, with a taller triangle giving a softer bite. For maximum braking power, position the straddle clamp 1½in to 2in (3.8 cm to 5.1 cm) from the rear tyre and the brake blocks as far forward in the clamps as possible.

4 Shimano straddle wires have a button-shaped junction that's marked for easy cable alignment. Pull the brake inner cable through until it aligns with the line on the button-shaped junction then firmly tighten the cantilever's cable clamp bolt.

5 Position the brake blocks approximately 2mm from the braking surface, then toe-in the leading edge of the block. Use paper folded over three times to get the gap at the trailing edge of the block. Check that there is at least 2mm of clearance between the blocks and the sidewall of the tyre when fully inflated, then tighten the brake blocks' clamp bolts.

6 Pull the brake lever back hard to seat and stretch the cable. Loosen and pull the cable through the anchor bolt if the brake lever comes back further than half way.

7 If a block drags on the rim, adjust the spring tension. Older style Shimano cantilevers use a tiny cross-headed or grub screw or Allen key; turn it clockwise to reduce drag on that arm, turn anti-clockwise if it's dragging on the other side. To adjust Dia Compe cantilevers very slightly, loosen the main 5mm Allen bolt then, using a cone spanner, turn the spanner away from the bike to increase tension. Finally, tighten the 5mm Allen bolt whilst holding the cone spanner in the same position.

ABOVE: Combined gear and brake levers, such as the STI unit shown here, can be used with either V-brakes or cantilevers.

LEFT: Straddle cables should be at 90 degrees to the cantilever arms, or as in this case aligned with the mark on the button-shaped junction.

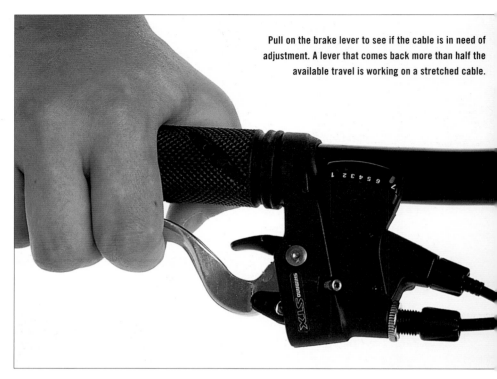

Pull on the brake lever to see if the cable is in need of adjustment. A lever that comes back more than half the available travel is working on a stretched cable.

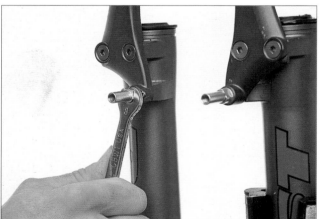

ABOVE: If the brakes persistently rub on one side, check that the bosses on the forks are tight.

Sorting your cantilevers

Grade of job: Easy

Tools: 5mm and 1.5mm Allen keys, spanners, sandpaper, pliers

• If the brake lever comes back more than half the available travel, the cable has stretched. Loosen the anchor bolt on the cantilever arm (it's usually a 5mm Allen bolt or 8mm nut) and draw the control cable through the anchor point with pliers. Leave about 2mm of space between the brake blocks and the rims on either side. Now tighten the anchor bolt fully.

Some cantilevers have small adjusting screws on the side of each arm.

Straddle wires need to be carefully adjusted using a pair of spanners.

• If your brake blocks are flat yet still rub on the rim go to step 7 on page 59.
The older style Shimano cantilevers mentioned there are adjusted using a 2mm Allen key that is available from most DIY and hardware stores.

If the brake block rubs on one side but releases itself when you turn the wheel, you have a wear o on the block. This is common after a wet ride or prolonged use and can be removed with a sharp knife, flat file or sandpaper.

Workshop notes

If you're fitting new cantilevers make sure all the bits are there and read the instructions carefully.

Sub-16in frames can have heel clearance problems. If you set up the cantilevers for maximum leverage replace the Shimano unit straddle for a conventional straddle clamp.

If the frame has just been re-finished make sure there's no paint on the cantilever boss. If there is, carefully remove with emery cloth and clean the boss thread with a 6mm-finishing tap.

disc brakes

Disc brakes have several advantages over traditional braking systems. These high-performance brakes are low maintenance, provide superior stopping power and are unaffected by the condition of a bike's wheel rim. The net effect is that the rider has more confidence in his brakes and, therefore, more confidence going into a turn or a descent.

Due to the weight of the rotor (disc) and the calipers, it is impossible to make a disc brake system that is as light as a typical V-brake set-up. However, despite this minor setback, discs are becoming increasingly popular on offroad bikes, including those intended for cross-country competition. Downhill bikes have long employed disc brakes, which are used to trim speed very rapidly. Disc brakes used on downhill bikes tend to be of bulkier construction than those used for general cross-country riding.

Disc maintenance

Maintaining disc brakes is quite simple as the mechanisms are sealed from the elements, and replacement brake pads can be fitted in a few minutes. Magura, Formula, Hope, Rock Shox and Diatech disc brake systems share the same fitting standard, so they are all compatible with the majority of suspension forks. However, it is worth noting that Manitou forks are intended for use with Hayes and Magura HS55 brake systems.

Different systems

Cable-operated disc brakes like the RST, Formula and Hayes brands use a 'worm drive' arrangement that presses the disc pads against the disc. Hydraulically operated disc brakes require more maintenance but are more effective where there is a long run between the caliper unit and the handlebar lever, for example on a downhill bike or an offroad tandem. The main service requirement is to keep the system free from air pockets, as this ensures that the handlebar control feels firm to operate at all times. When bleeding the system of air, fluid levels must be maintained to avoid the introduction off further air into the system. With the Hayes hydraulic system fresh fluid is fed from the top, while, by contrast, Hope brakes are bled by replenishing the fluid contained within a handlebar-mounted reservoir. Bleeding hydraulic brakes is basically the same for all systems.

Servicing Hope brakes

Grade of job: Moderate

Tools: 8mm wrench, screwdriver.

2 Attach a clear hose to the nipple on the caliper and place the other end of the hose into a vessel containing brake fluid. Make sure that the end of the hose is submerged in fluid.

1 Undo the reservoir cap while turning the adjuster screw on the cap anti-clockwise. Top-up the fluids in the reservoir then replace the cap.

3 Using an 8mm-wrench undo the bleed nipple slightly while gently squeezing on the handlebar brake lever.

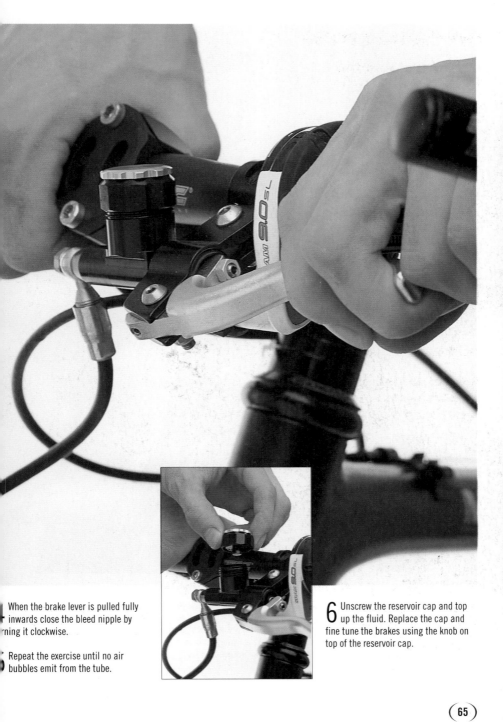

When the brake lever is pulled fully
inwards close the bleed nipple by
turning it clockwise.

Repeat the exercise until no air
bubbles emit from the tube.

6 Unscrew the reservoir cap and top
up the fluid. Replace the cap and
fine tune the brakes using the knob on
top of the reservoir cap.

Hydraulic brakes are extremely powerful but do require regular maintenance.

Servicing Hayes brakes

Grade of job: Difficult
Tools: 8mm wrench, screwdriver.

1 Loosen the brake lever and turn it so that the screw on the reservoir points upwards. Remove the screw. Place the cap on the end of the bleed hose and squeeze the bottle until all the air is expelled.

2 Press the end of the hose into the screw hole. Place another hose on the end of the caliper bleed nipple and put the other end into a bottle. Attach the bottle to the bike using tape in order to prevent it from falling over and spilling.

Hydraulic brake

Better known as the Magura Hydrostop, the Magura 'HS' range slide onto cantilever bosses using various fitting parts. This type of brake, which pre-dates disc brake systems, was the first to use a hydraulic operating system. The system remains popular and has garnered praise from trials riders and stunt specialists for its ability to modulate braking.

Fitting a Magura Hydrostop system to your bike is easy. The brakes can be purchased with a fitting kit that includes the hydraulic lines and olive shaped connectors (which form the seal between the line and the operating lever).

Grade of job: Moderate

Tools: adjustable spanner, screwdriver.

1 Trim the hydraulic line to the required length.

2 Place the nut over the line.

3 Place the copper olive over the line, fitting it the correct way round so that the flat line is facing the brake lever.

4 Carefully screw the hex nut together with the brake line into the brake cylinder assembly. Tighten the nut fully.

3 Depress the handlebar lever, and then simultaneously open the bleed pple using an 8mm-wrench. Close the pple and let go of the lever. At this age fluid from the bottle will plenish the reservoir.

4 Repeat the operation until no air bubbles emit from the tube attached to the caliper.

ABOVE: The screw inside the lever controls the point at which the brakes 'bite'.

BELOW: Snipe-nosed pliers are best employed to remove the pads from their calipers.

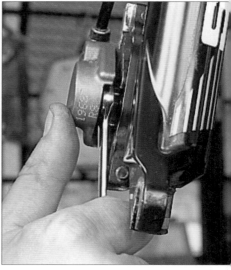

changing disc

LEFT: To centre the caliper mountings you will probably need an 'assistant' to pull the lever while you tighten the bolts.

LEFT: When tightening the caliper piston you must not blow dust away from the mechanism, as it may contain asbestos.

Grade of job: Moderate.

Tools: snipe-nosed pliers, 10mm spanner.

Disc brake pads have a much greater service life than traditional cantilever brake pads, which, when used in severe conditions can in a matter of hours wear down to the limit mark. Disc pads perform the same function as the replaceable brake blocks found on all 'V' type and cantilever brakes, but they have a much greater surface area to act upon. Changing the pads is simple as they are usually retained with a small clip inside the caliper unit. Here's how to change the pads in the Hayes system.

1 Ideally, place the bike on a workstand before removing the front wheel. Undo the nut on the end a few turns if the wheel seems stuck.

2 Pull both pads out of the caliper by their tabs. You will find it easier to use snipe-nosed pliers for this job.

3 Push the caliper piston inwards using a 10mm spanner. At this stage don't be tempted to blow any dust away as it may contain harmful asbestos particles.

4 The outer pad has an offset tab, and this must first be fitted at a slight angle, thus ensuring that the spring engages with the screw on the back of the piston. Once the spring is engaged, keep pushing the pad until it is fully home. Repeat this process for the inner brake pad.

5 With the pads in place, you must now centre the caliper mountings. Loosen the bolts holding the caliper to the forks, now squeeze the handlebar control while simultaneously tightening the two bolts you loosened earlier.

pads

ABOVE: Regular maintenance would have prevented the bearing cup on this pedal from becoming coroded.

RIGHT: The small bearing surface area of this axle means the bearing lands have worn rapidly.

maintaining clipped pedals

LEFT: Pedal components are tiny, so ensure that you put them all in a safe place when you strip a pedal.

Maintaining clipped pedals

Grade of job: Moderate
Tools required: Appropriate spanner or socket to remove locknut, vice, grease.

Clipped pedals are supplied as original equipment on most MTBs, but some, mainly the resin-bodied type, aren't sealed from the elements. In most cases, it is not worth stripping down resin-bodied pedals to repair them when the bearings become stiff. Firstly, the cageplates aren't removable, so it is often impossible to gain access to the bearings and, secondly, resin-bodied pedals are relatively cheap to replace. If, however, your pedals are of aluminium and steel construction, they are worth servicing for long life. To inspect the bearings follow the eight-point sequence below:

1 Unscrew the bolts that secure the cageplate and place the bolts in a safe place.

2 Prise off, or in the case of some pedals, screw off the end cap.

3 Place the pedal in a vice and, using the axle to hold it, turn the outermost axle nut anti-clockwise, followed by the tab washer and the adjuster cone.

4 Grasp the axle between thumb and forefinger, then remove the pedal from the jaws of the vice. Place the pedal into a plastic bag and invert it. The ball bearings will fall out, together with the axle. Clean and inspect the parts that the ball bearings run through, looking especially for pitting marks. The axle is most prone to problems.

5 Always fit new bearings; they cost little and the old ones will almost certainly have a degree of wear. Take the old ones to your bike shop to match replacements.

6 Use grease to hold the bearings in place. Position the axle on the vice and carefully place the pedal body over it. Replace the adjuster cone, turning it clockwise until it is just seated, then back it off a little. Fit the tab washer (where needed) and the locknut. Tighten the locknut fully, then grasp the pedal to check the bearings for play. If the bearings are tight or won't turn at all, loosen the locknut and turn the adjuster cone anti-clockwise a little. Tighten the locknut again. If the bearings have become loose, you will need to turn the adjuster cone clockwise.

7 If there isn't one already, drill a small hole about 1.5mm into the dustcap end of the pedal then apply some grease, squirting lubricant through the hole using a miniature grease gun.

8 If you are just re-greasing the pedals, pump the unit until all the old grease has been purged out from around the innermost part of the axle.

Jargon buster

Cageplate: This is the part that your soles grip.

Bearing lands: These are the parts of the pedal that the bearings run through. In this case, they are in the pedal body and the axle.

Adjuster cone: This is the bit that screws down the axle, allowing fine adjustment of the bearings.

maintaining SPD pedals

Tips

- When replacing the axle assembly into the right-hand pedal, turn the body of the pedal clockwise.

- If the pedal turns without unscrewing, the thread has stripped. Put the pedal axle in the vice and heat the body of the pedal using a butane torch. When the plastic bearing retainer starts to bubble, lift the pedal away from the axle, using molegrips. Avoid breathing the fumes. This procedure requires great care and should not be attempted by children.

- If you have to melt the axle assembly out find a well-ventilated area and open the windows, as the fumes are toxic.

- Don't try to remove the springs within the SPD mechanism – there's no need and it is extremely difficult to re-fit them.

- The four cross-headed retainer plate screws on XT SPDs have a habit of disappearing. Use a drop of glue on them to prevent them loosening.

- Use molegrips to hold the special tool if you don't have access to a vice; use your feet to stop the grips moving around.

Despite their diminutive size, the components of this pedal will provide years of service if regularly maintained.

Road bike clipless pedals seem to go on forever, but offroad versions require regular maintenance to keep their bearings running smoothly. The ubiquitous Shimano SPD pedal is covered here and yes, there is a use for that grey plastic ring that comes with the pedals.

LEFT: There should be no detectable play in the bearings. If there is, remove the axle assembly and (See step 2, right).

BOTTOM LEFT: Adjusting the bearings is a delicate but straightforward operation (See step 5, right).

RIGHT: Take great care when removing the axle bearings (See step 3, right).

BELOW: Using the special tool, turn the axle assembly into the body of the pedal. Place the tool in a vice and use the body of the pedal to tighten, but don't use excessive force.

Maintaining SPD pedals

Grade of job: Easy

Tools required: Vice or molegrips, 6mm and 10mm spanner, plastic bearings removal tool (included with Shimano pedals).

1 Clear the mud from the pedal using an old spoke and wash the remainder using degreaser.

2 Place the bearing removal tool (the grey plastic ring) over the right-hand pedal axle and cramp the tool in the jaws of a vice, then grasp the pedal body, turning it clockwise to unscrew the axle assembly. Turn the left-hand pedal anti-clockwise to remove the axle assembly.

3 Position the axle in the vice. Loosen the lock nut with a 6mm spanner, then loosen the tab washer and the cone. Place the bearing assembly in a container then lift the sleeve from the axle. The bearings will fall out. Inspect the bearing lands on the axle for serious pitting marks. Keep the bearing retainer sleeve, along with the axle you removed it from, and inspect the delicate plastic thread for damage. Replace with an aluminium version if there's damage or you've had to melt it to get the axle assembly out (see Tips).

4 Pop the plastic sleeve over the axle followed by the narrow washer, fit this with the chamfer uppermost, then apply a sticky grease (e.g., Mobil HP222 or Shimano Pro Line) to the axle and place the ³⁄₃₂in ball bearings around the washer. Slide the metal sleeve over the axle and place the plastic tube through it. Place further ³⁄₃₂in bearings around the outside edge of the sleeve, followed by the cone, tab washer and the locknut.

5 Using a 10mm spanner to hold the adjuster cone, adjust the bearings so that there is detectable play when the sleeve is moved. You can then tighten the locknut firmly, using a 6mm spanner.

6 Squeeze some grease into the pedal body before fitting the axle assembly. Carefully insert and screw in the axle (see Tips), then tighten firmly using the tool. If the bearings feel rough, remove the axle assembly and slacken the locking nut, then turn the adjuster cone about one eighth anti-clockwise. Finally, tighten the lock nut firmly down onto the adjuster cone.

fitting SPD cleats

Grade of job: Easy

Tools: screwdriver, knife.

There are two halves to a clipless pedal set-up: the pedals and the cleats. Correct fitting of the cleats to a pair of cycling shoes is vital, as misalignment can lead to knee problems. Most cycling shoes have a 'window' on the base of the sole for the fitting of cleats, however, this is merely a guide and the exact positioning of a cleat is down to individual preference. As a general rule, cleats should be aligned with the ball of the foot. Some cleats come in two versions: one where the cleat is fixed, and one where the foot can rotate by a few degrees (this feature is often called float). The latter variety is recommended for beginnners or riders who have sensitive knees. There are many brands of clipless pedals on the market, but the fitting of the cleats remains the same whichever model you choose.

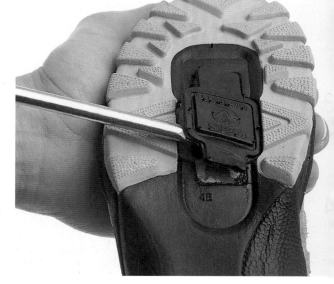

1 Cut out the square section (which is roughly 2cm long and adjacent to the ball of the foot) from the sole of the shoe using a sharp, short-bladed knife. Lever the section out from the shoe using a large flat screwdriver.

2 Some shoes come with a screw plate already fitted, but if yours do not, you will need to fit one. Remove the insole and place the screw plate into the shoe with the hole edges pointing downwards. Place the sticker over the plate to seal the shoe and replace the insole.

3 Put the shoe on and use a pen or correcting fluid to mark, on the sole, the position where the ball of your foot rests.

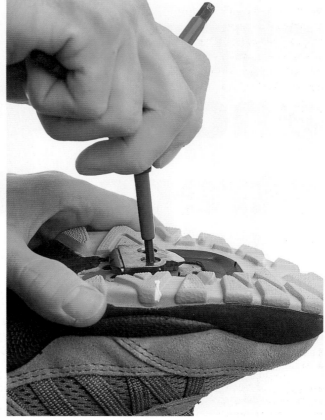

4 Remove the shoe and fit the cleats using the screws supplied. Apply a little oil to the threads and the heads of the screws before inserting them. Align the fitting screws with the mark that indicates the ball of your foot (see step 3) and tighten the screws firmly.

Road cyclists first used clips and straps more than one hundred years ago. Today, pedals are commonly made of a tough resin material while straps, which are constructed from a nylon weave, are extremely durable. The clips prevent the rider's feet from slipping forward and they allow the rider to adopt a circular pedalling motion, which is of particular benefit when climbing a hill.

fitting clips and straps

Grade of job: Easy
Tools required: None.

The majority of MTBs are supplied with traditional pedals complete with straps and clips. To make the best of such pedals, it is important to check that the straps are fiitted correctly.

The fear that your feet can get 'trapped' is unfounded as the strap's quick-release buckle frees the foot instantly when the force of the rider's

foot overcomes the spring tension in the buckle. The strap can be pulled up to increase the security of the feet in the clips, though the straps should be routed correctly to achieve maximum safety and comfort.

Here is the correct way to route the straps through the pedals and toe clips:

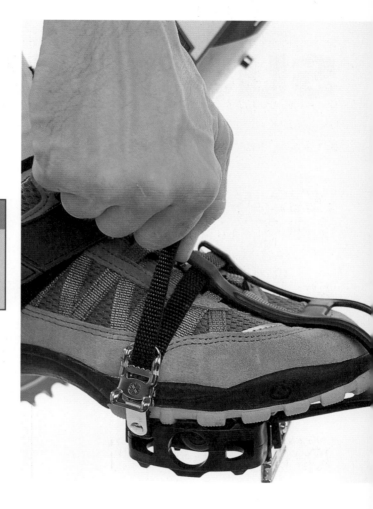

GHT: It is better to use proper
cling shoes rather than training
oes, as they fit more snugly into
ps and straps.

LOW, RIGHT: For your own safety
u should keep all the screws and
ts on your pedals tight.

With the buckle facing downwards, thread the end of the
strap through the slot in the outermost part of the pedal
ge and pull it through the cage.

With the buckle hard against the cage, twist the strap
once and thread it through the innermost part of the cage.

Loop the strap over and thread it through the hoop in the
toe clip.

Depress the strap buckle and thread the 'bare' end of the
strap through the gap in the buckle. The strap can now be
lled through to tension. Press the buckle to release the foot.

suspension

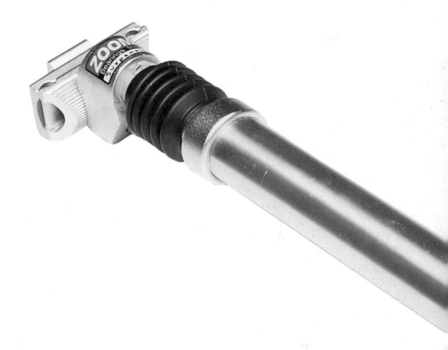

A suspension seatpost should be a priority upgrade on a hard tail bike. Seatposts of the telescoping kind consist of two tubes that slide into each other; they also contain multi-cellular units (MCUs) and wire springs, which provide the suspension. A new type of suspension seatpost has also emerged which consists of a parallelogram arrangement. Like suspension forks, you can alter the spring rate of a suspension seatpost by changing the springs or elastomers.

seatpost

The most frequent maintenance job on a suspension seatpost is the replacement of the pivot bushes. It is a simple job and requires nothing more taxing than removing several Allen bolts to gain access to the bushes. Specific maintenance instructions are usually supplied with the seatpost and these should be followed as a matter of course.

Regreasing a suspension seatpost

You can guard against wear by stripping, cleaning and regreasing the internal components regularly. At the very least do this whenever the action of the seatpost becomes noticeably less effective.

1. The upper and lower tubes are separated by a collar, unscrew this collar by hand and pull the upper part of the seatpost away from the bike to reveal the internal parts.

2. Remove all the old grease from the components and smear fresh grease on to them before reassembly.

solid seatpost and quick release bolts

To prevent movement the seatpost must fit tightly into the frame. Grease applied around the post will stop corrosion and prevent the post from sticking. Seatposts are only worth upgrading if your existing post is too short (there should be at least 2½in (6.35) of post within the seat tube).

Unseizing the seatpost. Remove the saddle and, using the frame as a lever, apply a twisting motion to free the seatpost.

Unseizing a seatpost

If your seatpost cannot be removed by manipulating the saddle, don't reach straight for the matches and the oxyacetylene torch... try the following approach first.

Grade of job: Difficult

Tools: large vice.

1 Remove the bottom bracket unit and, with the bike inverted, spray some freeing oil down the seat tube. Leave the oil to soak for at least 24 hours.

2 Remove both the wheels and the saddle, then clamp the top of the seatpost in the jaws of a vice. If the seatpost has a separate steel saddle clasp, cut the narrow section at the top and place a short piece of steel rod or a socket into the tube, before clamping the seatpost. Using the frame as a lever, turn and lift the bike simultaneously to release the seatpost. If this doesn't work, strip the bike entirely, after which the frame will have to be entrusted to a frame builder who will melt the seatpost out of the frame using a torch. In this case, the bike may need a respray as the heat used will affect the paintwork.

3 Before fitting a replacement seatpost, coat the outside surface with an anti-seize compound or grease. Fresh grease should be applied every three months.

th the thumbscrew in the left hand and the quick-release lever in the right
nd, turn the thumbscrew until the lever is in line with the wheel axle. Gently
ess the lever and turn the thumbscrew in a clockwise direction to take up
y slack.

Quick release bolts

Cyclists often misuse quick-release mechanisms, but it is important to use these devices properly for your own safety. Quick-release skewers come in many shapes and colours, but all do the same job of securing the wheels to the frame. Lightweight skewers can be bought as an upgrade but aren't as cost effective as substituting heavy tyres for those with a Kevlar bead, for instance.

Tip

- If you need a longer seatpost be sure to state the diameter required. There are many different sizes of tube on the market, and each should be stamped with its dimensions. If your post isn't marked, seek advice from a bike shop.

th the lever in line with the wheel axle, press the lever fully home using the
m of the hand. Do not push the lever right up against the fork, as doing so
l make it difficult to later remove the wheel.

handlebars

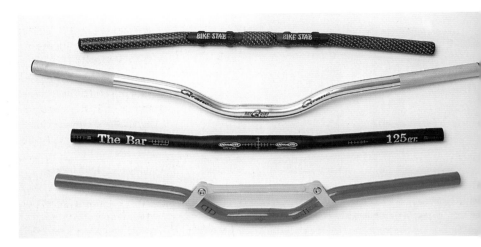

Tip

- The force exerted on a bar end during a spill can result in a crimped handlebar. The damaged portion of the tube can be trimmed with a hacksaw though, of course, this narrows your bars considerably.

- To avoid confusion when ordering a new quill stem, look for the size stamped on the stem, 25.4mm refers to 1in, 30.2mm refers to 1⅛in and there's Evolution 1¼in. A-head stems are available in either 1in or 1⅛in.

Handlebar reach is a matter of personal preference, though as a guide weight should be evenly distributed between the saddle and the handlebar. There is a vast range of stems available, all of which will effect your riding position and thereby comfort. Whatever set-up you choose, aim to get a position that's comfortable on the grips and on bar ends too.

MTB manufacturers have spent years getting the handlebar set-up right for the mass market and, provided your bike shop has advised you correctly regarding the size of bike, you're uunlikely to gain any significant advantage by changing the manufacturer's stem. Downhill racers favour a stem that's usually 3cm shorter than a cross-country stem.

and stems

ABOVE AND LEFT: Handlebars and bar-ends come in a variety of materials and designs, although fashion seems to motivate more upgrades than practical considerations.

Inspection and stem replacement

Grade of job: Moderate

Tools: 5mm and 6mm Allen keys, screwdriver, spray oil or washing-up liquid, Copper Eze or waterproof grease.

1 If a stem is cracked as a result of an accident, inspect all welds closely for similar damage.

2 Remove the grips. Poke a screwdriver behind the grip and squirt with a thin lube, work the blade round the grip and pull with a twisting motion. Remove the brake and gear levers.

3 To remove an A-head type stem, undo the top Allen bolt followed by the side bolt, lift the stem and handlebar assembly from the fork steerer and take care not to lose the spacers if fitted.

4 To remove a quill-type stem leave the handlebar in position, turn the Allen head bolt anti-clockwise and lift the handlebar/stem assembly together.

5 To fit a new A-head stem, use the correct number of spacer washers to achieve the correct fork steerer overlap. Fit the handlebars and controls and tighten them enough to prevent them turning – though no further.

6 Quill stems should be greased before fitting. Coat the sliding surfaces of the wedge, the threads of the bolt and the underside of the bolt head. Don't forget to coat the outside of the wedge to prevent corrosion.

wedging the stem open with a large screwdriver you prevent scratching the handlebars. Never force the handlebars into a tight stem. If in doubt get advice regarding compatibility from a reputable shop.

the headset

The headset controls the movement of the fork. It contains ball bearings or roller bearings that must be kept properly adjusted for the steering to remain true. There are two basic types of headset: the threaded type, which fit onto a fork with a threaded steerer tube, and the threadless kind, which adjust by Allen bolt.

Use an Allen key (usually a 6mm key) to secure the stem to the fork steerer.

Threadless headset (cut away)

Threaded headset (cut away)

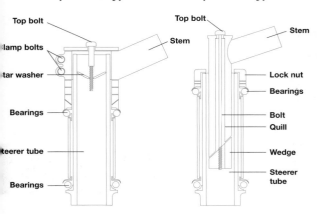

Threadless headset labels:
- Top bolt
- Clamp bolts
- Star washer
- Bearings
- Steerer tube
- Bearings

Threaded headset labels:
- Top bolt
- Stem
- Lock nut
- Bearings
- Bolt
- Quill
- Wedge
- Steerer tube

ABOVE: Neoprene headset protectors help prolong the life of a headset.

ABOVE: When reassembled correctly, the headset should work smoothly.

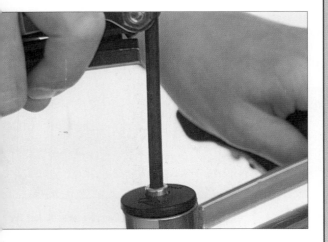

Use a 5mm Allen key to remove any detectable play in the steering.

Headset adjustment

Grade of job: Moderate

Tools: 6mm and 5mm Allen keys (threadless headset), headset spanners (conventional headsets).

Threaded headset

1 Place your thumb and forefinger around the lower stack of the headset, then, using your right hand, apply the front brake and push fore and aft. If there is play detectable, slacken the uppermost nut on the headset stack, then turn the nut beneath it clockwise until you feel resistance.

2 Using a spanner to hold the lower nut in position, tighten the upper nut down onto the lower nut. Keeping the upper nut stationary, turn the lower nut anti-clockwise until it will move no further.

Threadless headset

1 The most commonly used threadless headset has a 5mm bolt in the top and usually a 5mm Allen-headed side bolt.

2 If you can detect play using the same method as described in step 1 for the threaded headset, slacken the side bolt, then turn the top bolt about one-eighth of a turn. Check that your handlebars are straight before fully tightening the side bolt.

Many older style forks require frequent maintenance, as they are prone to wear due to damp getting into the sliding components. More recent designs, however, have effective weather sealing arrangements. It is best to service the fork using a workstand, although you can leave it on the bike. Keep the forks vertical as the parts can easily fall out.

Fork specifications and service intervals vary widely from model to model. The information given in this book is merely a guide and should be used in conjunction with specific instructions, obtained from either a reputable bike shop or manufacturer.

Some forks use elastomers for both springing and damping action, while others use springs combined with oil for damping. The RST

Changing colour

Changing the elastomers in suspension forks can make a bigger difference to the spring rate. The elastomers are colour coded and, for RST forks, the colours work as follows:
Cream = softest
Blue = intermediate
Red = hardest

suspension

forks illustrated here have a spring to provide initial take-up when you sit on the bike, but they are classed as an elastomer fork. Elastomer forks rely on grease for smooth running, so regular replenishment of their grease is vital to ensure smooth operation.

Adjusting elastomer forks

Elastomer forks can be tuned for better performance. For example, to improve compliance on small bumps and slightly increase travel, you should remove one of the spacer washers in each leg. Similarly, by turning the plastic knob at the top of the fork legs clockwise, you can increase the amount of force required to move the fork.

Attach a cable tie to the fork leg in order to determine how far the suspension travels.

Basic service

Grade of job: Difficult

Tools: Allen keys, flat bladed screwdriver, grease.

1 Remove the Allen bolt in the base of the lower leg. Compress the forks if the bolts turn but do not actually loosen.

2 Slacken the 5mm Allen bolts in the crown then unscrew the plastic knob at the top of each fork leg.

orks

4 Separate the lower forks from the uppers by employing a tugging action.

5 Clean the fork wiper seals on the top of the lower part of the fork. Clean all the internal components.

3 Lift out the elastomer stack on the kebab-like damper rod.

6 Grease the components individually and replace them in the same order that they came off the rod. Apply grease to the lower tube using a piece of dowel rod.

Grade of job: Easy

Tools: Zip tie, oil.

It is worth taking the time to adjust your forks as it will make the ride smoother and prolong the life of the forks. A tip for increasing the amount of suspension travel on elastomer forks is to remove one of the spacer washers in each leg, this will improve compliance on small bumps and increase travel slightly. Changing the elastomers makes a bigger difference to the spring rate. Some forks, e.g., the Rock Shox Judy, have separate damping cartridges to suit rider weight and terrain.

tuning suspension forks

Steerer tubes

Pre-load adjuster

Elastomer

Spacer

Spring

Tubes or stanchions

Damper Rod

Bottom-out bumpers

Fork boots

Cantilever brake bosses

Fork lower legs or fork slider

Exploded fork

Damping adjuster bolt

Basic adjustments

1 When you sit on the bike the forks will sag. You can measure the degree of sag by attaching a cable tie to one of the upper fork legs. When you've attached it press it flush with the oil seal. By turning the plastic knob on the top of the fork you can alter the amount of sag to your requirements. You may find it better to change the spring if, with the adjuster turned fully clockwise, more than 20 per cent of the total travel is taken up by the initial sag.

2 To establish the total suspension travel available, compress the fork and observe the position of the zip tie you attached earlier. If, when you ride offroad, the fork is constantly moving to its limit, you should change the spring for one of a harder grade.

3 Some forks have damping adjustment screws. These alter the speed at which the fork reacts to the terrain. Turning the plastic knob at the top of the fork legs clockwise increases the amount of force required to move the fork.

4 Some fork manufacturers recommend that you apply a little oil to the fork seals before every ride. Lubrication will help prevent 'stiction', which is caused by friction between the sliding components. Lift the upper boots and apply a dry lube.

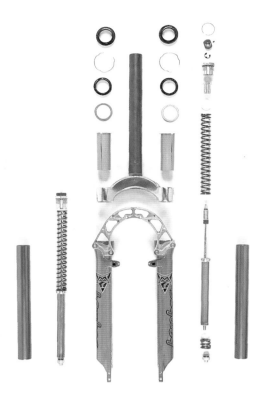

RIGHT: Take care when removing the top cap as the damper assembly can unexpectedly spring out.

FAR RIGHT: Fill your forks with the correct oil. Check with a bike shop if you are unsure which oil to use.

servicing air-oil forks

Grade of job: Difficult

Tools: screwdriver, socket wrench and sockets.

Air-oil forks are sealed from the outside world, but their internal moving parts are bathed in oil so they are supplied with a constant degree of lubrication. In time, the oil thins, becomes contaminated with metallic particles and requires replacement. The job of the oil seals is to contain the oil within the forks while the lower and upper fork tubes telescope into each other. Sometimes the seals wear, allowing grit to get behind the seal, thereby causing oil and air leaks (if the fork uses air as a spring).

Here is how to service an air-oil fork, using the Marzocchi Bomber as an example.

1 Unscrew the protective plastic top cap from the upper fork and prise off the circlips using a screwdriver. Hold the fork away from you as the spring could push the damper assembly out.

2 Lift the damper assembly out of the fork and pour the oil out.

3 Turn to the bottom of the lower fork and undo the nut using a socket wrench.

4 Separate the upper and lower fork legs.

5 Turn the upper leg upside down to withdraw the rebound spring.

6 Clean all internal parts using white spirit or an eco-friendly cleaner.

7 If the forks have been leaking, prise off the fork seal using a large flat screwdriver and replace with new seals.

8 Reassemble the parts, then fill with SAE 7.5 oil to a point 40mm from the top of each leg.

9 Inspect the 'o' ring on the damper assembly before fitting it into the top of each tube followed by the snap ring. Inflate each tube using the special pump to 1.8–2.2 bar pressure. Now fit the dust cap.

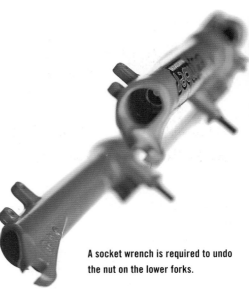

A socket wrench is required to undo the nut on the lower forks.

looking after

Frame protection

You can protect the unpainted insides of your MTB's frame with an automotive underbody sealant compound of the type that flows freely into crevices.

Grade of job: Moderate

Tools: drill, screwdriver, tape.

1 Remove the bottom bracket unit (b/b) and forks.

2 Centre-punch the b/b shell and use a small starter drill. Then use a larger drill to at least ⅛in. Remove the burr on the inside of the b/b shell with a file or a blunt screwdriver.

3 Stuff newspaper into the business end of the seat tube and a piece of tape across the two vent holes inside the head tube.

4 With the bike upside-down place the straw, which comes with the sealant, inside the seat tube and depress spray for about seven seconds. Repeat inside the down tube and chainstays. Stuff more newspaper into the b/b shell and turn the frame a few times to disperse the sealant evenly. Remove the newspaper and stand for at least two days to allow any excess to drain from the frame tubing before reassembly.

Touch up the paintwork

Inevitably, chips appear in paintwork. It's unavoidable but easy to touch up, and it's important to do so before corrosion gets a hold.

1. Find a colour sample that is similar to that of your bike. Take it to an automotive supplier who will be able to get a close match with a tube of touch-up paint.

2. Wipe the area to be touched up with thinners then apply a small dab of paint to the area. Leave to dry before applying further dabs of paint until the touch up layers are higher than the rest of the paint.

3. Using wet-and-dry sandpaper, lightly sand your touch-up until it's flush with the rest of the paint, then use a light rubbing compound to shine.

If you can't get the right colour to touch up your paintwork, use nail varnish instead.

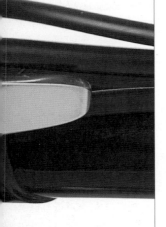

Damage to the chainstays

Examine the area of your frame adjacent to the chainrings. Damage can occur here due to 'chainsuck'. This is where the chain jams in the chainring teeth, and gets stuck between the frame and the chainring. A special device can reduce the chance of damage should this happen on your bike. There are several brands of anti-chainsuck device on the market.

Protect the insides of your frame by using an automotive underbody compound.

full suspension

ABOVE: Regularly inspect the moving parts of the frame for wear and cracks.

RIGHT: Most
friction bearing
parts on a dual
suspension
frame are
replaceable.

Leave the maintenance of suspension units to the experts

The quest for stronger and lighter materials has seen carbon fibre bikes become commonplace. The all-carbon GT STS and the Schwinn 4 Banger (shown here), which has a carbon rear end, are just two of many examples.

The GT LTS is a clear example of a system that requires regular maintenance in order to prevent premature wear of the moving components. Always ask your dealer about maintenance intervals before you purchase a new frame, but leave any work on the suspension unit itself to a specialist. Suspension units are gas filled and, if tampered with, can explode.

The staff at your local bike shop should also be able to advise you on whether you will need any special tools to service the moving parts yourself. You will usually obtain better access to the components by first removing the chainset and moving the front mech out of the way. Suspension arms and the associated linkages are generally supported by a central pin,

rames

Modern suspension forks, with their increased travel and length, place an increased stress on the tubing. Gussets are built into most suspension frames to handle the strain. These gussets can usually be found beneath the down tube and behind the head tube.

hich must be drifted out to ain access to the moving parts, ut be careful to ensure that any etaining bolts are first loosened efore attempting to remove the in. Kits containing replacement arts are usually available hrough your local retailer. Use lenty of grease upon eassembly and, most nportantly, ensure bolts are ghtened using the manufacturer's recommended orque settings.

ABOVE: Make sure that you replace all seals upon reassembly of a suspension frame. The seals are seen here draped over the suspension arms.

getting your bike resprayed

A respray can make your MTB look like new. It will also reveal any flaws or cracks in your frame that my lie beneath the old paintwork.

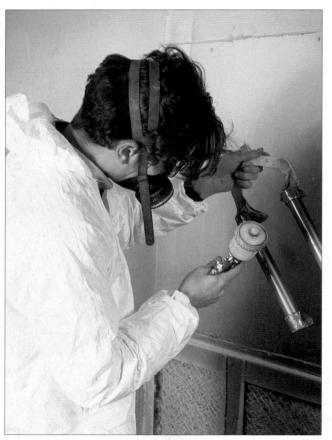

The downside, however, is that resprays are expensive, although significant savings can be made by dismantling the bike yourself. Most frame builders and larger cycle retailers have paint facilities. You will usually be given a colour chart showing you what paints are available at what price. Some finishers can match a shade from your reference, which could be anything from a colour swatch card to a crisp packet.

The frame and forks must be completely degreased before the respraying process can begin. Next, old paint is removed from the frame by one of two

LEFT: Suspension forks can be sprayed and finished to match the frame.

RIGHT: These frames have been painted but await the application of a coat of protective lacquer.

ocesses. Steel frames are
ndblasted to leave the bare
etal exposed. Painted
minium frames require a
ore delicate method of
eatment, as the tubing material
too soft to withstand the
fects of a sandblaster. Old
int is removed using a
emical treatment followed by
ight sandblast. The
ndblasting provides a key for
the new paint to adhere to.
Once all old paint is removed,
the frame can be inspected for
cracks and any other problems
that may have been concealed.

The paint is then sprayed
onto the frame in several coats.
Transfers are applied to the
painted frame followed by a
coat of lacquer. The frame is
then placed into an oven to fully
harden the paint.

Tip

You can protect the
paintwork on your frame by
applying adhesive plastic
pads. These can be placed
where the cables rub on the
paintwork.

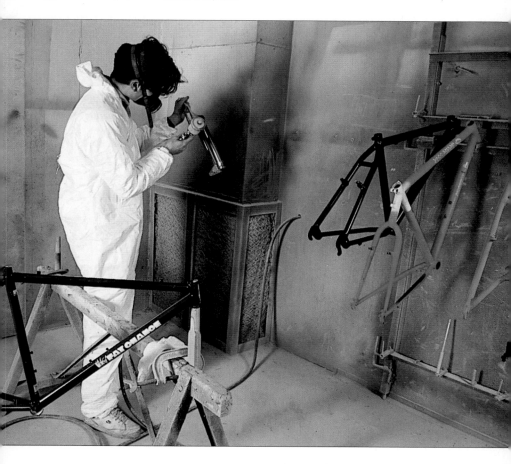

troubleshooting

Symptom	Cause
Saddle soreness	Saddle not level/Wrong type of saddle
Bike uncomfortable	Cramped or stretched position
Wrists ache	Cramped position
Bike feels vague and difficult to steer	Tight steering bearings or loose spokes
Gears click	Cable stretched
Chain won't go onto small chainring	Maladjusted gear
Chain falls off repeatedly	Maladjusted gear
Bike vibrates when brakes applied	Dented or out of true wheel
Squeaking noise on each pedal revolution	Loose crank arm
Light click on each pedal revolution	Stiff chain link
Frequent punctures	Insufficient air in tyres/Foreign object in tyre ca
Knocking noise over uneven surfaces	Headset loose
Bike pulls to one side	Forks or possibly frame bent

emedy

oosen clamp and adjust until level/Change saddle

ove saddle or change the stem

nange the stem

djust steering. Adjust spoke tension

ull cable through gear mech

djust low limit gear screw

djust low or high limit screw

ue wheel using spoke key

ghten crank

anipulate the chain with your thumbs or use the upper portion of a chain tool

late tyres and use tyre gauge/Remove foreign objects with a dull knife blade

djust using headset spanner

ew frame/forks or change the stem

silence unwanted noises

Rattles and jingles caused, for example, by loose change in a seatpack or the chain slapping on the frame are normal. Other noises can signal problems. Below are some common unwanted noises along with solutions to silence the squeals.

Noise: Squeaky noise coming from the rear of the bike.
Solution: The most common cause of a high pitched continuous or rhythmical squeaking sound is the freewheel. Apply oil to the area immediately between the spokes and the rear wheel cogs to remedy this problem.

Noise: Loud squeak on every pedal revolution.
Solution: This is usually caused by a loose interface between the pedal crank arms and the bottom-bracket axle. Tighten the bolt which secures the crank arm to the axle quite firmly; it should be 22ft/lb if you are using a torque wrench.

Noise: Faint clicking sound on, approximately, every three revolutions of the pedals.
Solution: The chain is very prone to corrosion and so this noise could indicate a stiff link. Pedal the cranks backwards and watch where the chain passes through the rear mech. A stiff link here will be immediately apparent. Manipulate the links with your hands to free up the offending link, or use a chain tool and then oil the chain.

Keep your chain well lubricated and check it regularly for corroded links.

Noise: Barely discernible scuffing sound.
Solution: The brake blocks may be rubbing on the sidewall of the tyre. This is very commonly associated with damage to the wheel rims and must be sorted immediately if damage to the tyre is to be avoided. Using a 5mm Allen key together with a 10mm spanner, loosen and readjust the brake blocks to avoid contact with the tyre all the way around the rim.

Noise: Knocking sound when suspension forks compress.
Solution: To check for worn fork bushes apply the front brake while grasping the area between the fork's lower and upper tubes. Visit your local retailer for further advice if movement here is accompanied by a pronounced knocking sound when you traverse bumps.

ten top tips

Making your mountain biking safer and more enjoyabl

1 For maximum night riding safety, ensure that the connections to your lights are tight. If necessary tape any wires in place and make sure that bottle cage mounted battery units are firmly secured and fully charged.

2 Make cleaning your MTB easier by giving the whole bike a coating of oil or, if you have got the time, car body wax. This will make it difficult for mud to grip onto your bike.

3 Apply grease to any bolts before assembling a component such as a seatpost clamp or stem wedge, as this will make future adjustments easier to carry out.

4 After a ride in muddy conditions don't leave your bike overnight before cleaning it. In the space of 24 hours, the chain will already have begun to rust. Dirt and grime will also quickly begin penetrating gears and suspension.

5 Never half tighten a component with the intention of coming back to the job later. You may forget and ride off with a vital component loose. At best the bike will be damaged and at worst, you wi be too.

6 Don't ride a full suspensio bike that has a known crack in the frame or sub assembly. Get the part replace if it is under warranty or buy a replacement.

7 The fitting of a chain guide can eliminate the annoying ound the chain makes when it lams against the frame. The implest chain guide is the DCD.

8 If you are transporting your bike use a chainstay rotector.

9 Preserve your expensive knobbly tyres for the trail. Fit licks if you intend to ride on the oad for a while, as they will roll nore efficiently.

10 Clip-on mudguards protect you and your bike om the dirt.

get you home tips

With improvisation, these 'get you home' tips can salvage a day's riding. It is essential to take a pump everywhere and to replace the spare inner tube you used last time you had a 'flat'. Here are the five most frequently encountered problems and their answers.

1. Fork and frame bent

To repair this problem, you will need a helper. Remove the front wheel, and then place the fork ends into the slots of a roadsid storm drain. You and your help must stand face to face and pu the rear of the bike upwards ar back to 'stretch' the forks straight.
Time: 10-20 minutes
Difficulty: Moderate

2. Bent rear mech

Grasp the cageplate and bend back with your hands until straight. You will find the cageplate easier to lever using screwdriver. Adjust the mech t avoid clashing with the spokes first gear.
Time: 20-30 minutes
Difficulty: Moderate

3. Buckled wheel

It is usually possible to straighten out a rim at the side of the trail. Remove the tyre and tube then look across the rim to establish where the bend occurs in the rim. Hold the rim very firmly either side of the dent then strike the bent portion very hard against the ground. If the rim doesn't succumb to your efforts loosen the spokes adjacent to the damage and try again.

Time: 15-30 minutes
Difficulty: Hard

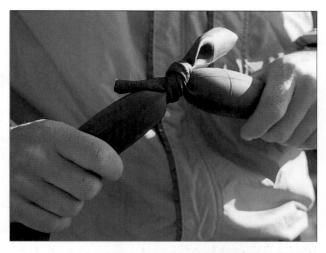

4. Blown inner tube

If you are in the middle of nowhere and one of your inner tube explodes, don't worry. Remove the tyre and tube then tie the ends together very tightly. Partially inflate the inner tube and feed it into the tyre. Now inflate to half recommended pressure, which for an MTB tyre is around 20 psi.

Time: 20-30 minutes
Difficulty: Moderate

5. Broken chain

A broken chain caused by sideplates splaying is a common problem. The solution is to shorten the chain by a couple of links. If you don't have a chain tool, place a piece of fencing wire through the sideplate. Use a small gear or ratchet the pedals if the new link grinds through the pedals.

Time: 10-15 minutes
Difficulty: Moderate

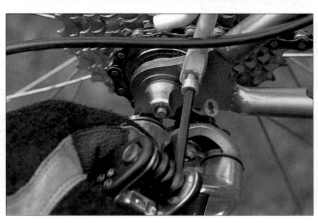

During the winter months your mountain bike is more likely to develop problems if you neglect maintenance. Take these steps to halt wear and corrosion.

winte

Frame patches

Protect expensive paintwork from scratches with frame patches. Patches should be positioned where cables run near or against the frame.

Grunge Guard

Grunge guards fit over Shimano front and rear gear mechs. They are highly recommended as the shield the moving parts of the gear mechanisms from trail borr water and dirt.

Securing grips

Grips have a tendency to slip around the handlebar in wet weather, when moisture creeps behind the rubber. Paint the bars and the inside of the grips with touch-up paint or hair spray, then slide the grip over the handlebars

precautions

Crud Claw

This little widget is available from good cycle retailers. It stops the chain from jumping when riding in severe, muddy conditions by preventing the build up of dirt between the sprockets.

Headset

The headset is particularly vulnerable to moisture penetration during the winter months. Protect the bearings with a neoprene headset cover. Alternatively, a section of old inner tube can be stretched over the lower headset race for protection.

Grease the seatpost

Moisture can get down between the seatpost and the frame causing the seatpost to fuse itself to the frame. Prevent this by the regular application of silicon-based or copper grease.

Fitting mudguards

Along with the protection they provide in wet weather, clip-on mudguards provide sufficient mud clearance for offroad use.

glossary

alloy A mixture of metals. Steel can be used alloyed (as *chromoly*) or on its own – though it is rather heavy like this. Lighter metals such as aluminium and titanium must be alloyed to improve strength.

b

bearings Bikes use ball bearings of various sizes in the headset, hub axles, freewheel, pedals and bottom bracket. Sometimes they're loose, sometimes set in a cage or race.

braze-ons Non-structural 'extras' on a frame, including bosses for bottle cages or gear levers, and eyelets for racks or mudguards.

brazing Like soldering, but a lot hotter, brazing joins two steel surfaces together with another metal that has a lower melting point, such as brass.

butted tubing Tubing which is internally thicker at the stressed tube ends than in the middle. It gives the same strength tube for less weight. Spokes may also be butted.

c

cartridge Cartridge bearings are generally used on expensive MTB components such as the headset and bottom bracket. Many suspension forks have cartridge damper units to enable speedy alteration of the damping characteristics of the forks.

caliper In the case of a disc-braking system, the calipers are the components that act against the flat steel-discs to stop the bike.

chromoly Steel alloyed with chrome and molybdenum, giving greater strength for less weight.

cleat Metal or plastic plate used to lock a cycle shoe to the pedal.

clipless pedals Pedals with sprung, ski-type bindings, which lock a dedicated cleat to the pedal. As a rule, clipless pedals cannot be ridden with ordinary shoes. MTB Clipless pedals are double-sided.

crank The lever that connects the pedal to the bottom bracket and the chainring.

chainguide Used on downhill bikes to stop the chain jumping off the chainring.

d

dished wheel Derailleur-geared rear wheels are dished, meaning the spokes on the cassette side are shorter and angled moore steeply than on the other side so that there is room for the cassette between the dropouts. Front wheels are symmetrical.

dropouts Where the wheel axles bolt into the frame.

astomers These are the rubber doughnut-like
acer/springs that form part of the internal workings of
stomer suspension forks. Elastomers are colour-coded
ording to their spring rate (hard to soft).

ehub A hub with an integral freewheel. Also known as a
ssette hub.

ewheel Mechanism of bearings, pawls and ratchets.
en freewheeling (rolling without pedalling), the pawls slide
er the ratchets, giving a distinctive clicking sound. When
dalling, the pawls engage the ratchets, driving the wheel.
ew-on freewheels have been made almost obsolete by
ehubs.

oupset The gear shifters, derailleurs, cassette, hubs,
akes, brake levers and sometimes the chainrings and
anks.

aitor The protective shroud found on some suspension
ks and seatposts.

ub flange The shoulder of the hub, where the holes for
e spokes are located.

ard tail Bike with no rear suspension.

dex gearing Click-up, click-down gearing.

gs Pre-cut metal joints into which tubes are brazed during
ame making.

ech Short for mechanism - there's a front and rear mech
your bike.

n

nipple On a spoke, the nipple is a threaded collar that
screws onto the spoke on the inner side of the rim. Turning the
nipple tightens or loosens the spoke by drawing more or less
of it through the rim.

p

pre-load This is referred to in the suspension systems as
the amount of spring that's already compressed inside the fork
– increasing the pre-load makes the fork harder to compress.

r

rake Rake is the distance between a line drawn through the
steerer tube and a parallel line drawn through the front
dropouts. It largely determines the MTB's steering
characteristics.

s

spider The spider-shaped (or spider-with-legs-missing-
shaped) end of the right-hand crank.

steerer tube Threaded upper end of the front fork, which
goes inside the head tube.

stem Clamp-fixing component which joins the steerer tube
and the handlebars.

shock Rear suspension unit.

swinging arm The rear section of a dual suspension frame.

t

TIG welding Short for tungsten inert gas welding. TIG
welding melts two tubes directly together without a joining
material.

v

V-Daptor This little device makes older style handlebar
control levers compatible with the V-brake arms.

viscosity The 'w' (or weight) refers to the thickness of a
grade of oil-i.e. 5w oil is thinner than 10w.

index

Acknowledgements

In source order

Octopus Publishing Group Ltd./Mark
Winwood Front Jacket insert, / Tim
Woodcock Front Cover, Back Cover, 1, 2-
3, 4-5, 6, 7, 8-9, 10, 11, 12, 13 Top, 13
Bottom Right, 14-15, 16 left, 16 right, 17
Top, 17 Bottom, 18 Top Right, 18 Bottom
Left, 19 Top, 19 Bottom, 20 left, 20 right,
21 Top, 21 Bottom, 22, 23, 24, 25, 26-
27, 27, 28, 28-29 Bottom, 29 Top Right,
29 Centre Right, 30, 31 Bottom Left, 31
Top Right, 32-33, 33 Top Right, 34 Top
Right, 34 Bottom, 35, 36, 37 Top, 37
Bottom, 38 Top Left, 38 Bottom Left, 39
Top Left, 39 Top Centre, 39 Top Right,
40-41 Bottom, 41 Top Right, 41 Bottom
Right, 42, 43 Top, 43 Bottom Left, 43
Bottom Right, 44 Top Right, 44 Bottom
Left, 45 Bottom Right, 46, 47, 48, 49 Top
Left, 49 Bottom, 50, 51 Top, 51 Bottom,
52, 53 Top, 53 Bottom, 54-55 Main
Picture, 55 Top Left, 55 Top Right, 56
Bottom Left, 56 Bottom Right, 57, 58, 59
left, 59 right, 60 Top, 60 Bottom, 61 Top,
61 Bottom, 63, 64 left, 64 Top Right, 64
Bottom Right, 65 Main Picture, 65 insert
bottom, 66 right, 66 Top Left, 66 Bottom
Left, 67, 68 Top Left, 68 Bottom Left, 68-
69 Top Centre, 68-69 Bottom Centre, 69
Bottom Right, 70 Top Left, 70 Top Right,
70 Bottom Right, 71 Top Left, 72 Top
Centre, 72 Centre, 72 Bottom Centre, 73
Top, 73 Bottom, 74, 75 left, 75 Top Right,
75 Bottom Right, 76, 77 Top, 77 Bottom,
78-79 Main Picture, 79, 80, 81 Top, 81
Bottom, 82, 83 Top, 83 Bottom, 84, 85
Top, 85 Bottom, 86, 87 Top, 87 Bottom
Left, 87 Bottom Right, 89 Top Left, 89
Top Right, 89 Bottom Left, 89 Bottom
Right, 90 Top Left, 90-91 Top, 91 Top
Right, 91 Bottom Right, 92-93 Main
Picture, 93 Bottom Right, 94 Top Left, 94
Bottom, 95, 96, 97, 98, 99 Top Left, 99
Top Right, 100-101, 102 Top, 103 Top
Right, 103 Centre Right, 104, 105 Top
Right, 105 Centre Right, 105 Bottom
Right, 106 Top, 106 Bottom Left, 107 Top
Right, 107 Bottom Right, 108.